Global Software Development

Managing Virtual Teams and Environments

Dale Walter Karolak

IEEE
COMPUTER SOCIETY

Los Alamitos, California

Washington • Brussels • Tokyo

Library of Congress Cataloging-in-Publication Data

Karolak, Dale Walter.
    Global software development: managing virtual teams and
environments / Dale Walter Karolak.
        p.   cm.
        ISBN 0-8186-8701-0
        1. Computer software – Development – Management.   I. Title.
QA76.76.D47K365   1998
005.1 '068 — dc21

                                                                98-43201
                                                                CIP

IEEE Computer Society Press Order Number BP08701
Library of Congress Number 98-43201
ISBN 0-8186-8701-0

Additional copies may be ordered from:

IEEE Computer Society Press
Customer Service Center
10662 Los Vaqueros Circle
P.O. Box 3014
Los Alamitos, CA 90720-1314
Tel: +1-714-821-8380
Fax: +1-714-821-4641
Email: cs.books@computer.org

IEEE Service Center
445 Hoes Lane
P.O. Box 1331
Piscataway, NJ 08855-1331
Tel: +1-732-981-0060
Fax: +1-732-981-9667
mis.custserv@computer.org

IEEE Computer Society
Watanabe Building
1-4-2 Minami-Aoyama
Minato-ku, Tokyo 107-0062
JAPAN
Tel: +81-3-3408-3118
Fax: +81-3-3408-3553
tokyo.ofc@computer.org

Publisher: Matt Loeb
Project Editor: Cheryl Baltes
Advertising/Promotions: Tom Fink

IEEE
COMPUTER
SOCIETY
IEEE

Acknowledgments

The following people deserve special thanks for their help and support

- To my wife, Lorraine, and our children, Ryan and Christine, for your patience while I was writing late into many nights.

- To TRW and my past employers, who have given me rich experiences and countless learning opportunities.

- To my friends at the Union Institute, who taught me what lifelong learning is all about.

- To my special friends, who continued to provide motivation and encouragement in completing this manuscript.

- To Allan Vogele who contributed to my knowledge about patent processes.

- To Kurt Buesching for his design of the book's cover.

Contents

Preface

It is becoming increasingly harder to justify completing a software development project inside company walls. As the software community begins to appreciate the economy of merging diverse development skills and domain expertise, and as communication media become more sophisticated, the cost and technology pressures are pushing more companies toward virtual projects: It is becoming less and less cost-effective or competitive to develop a software product in the same building, company, or even country. Former obstacles—the lack of mature processes, the prevalence of nonstandard computer languages, unstable communication, and tools with poor integration capabilities—are shrinking in importance. Although software development engineering is still far from a mature discipline, improvements in tools and methods over the last several decades are allowing groups from different locations and cultures and with different expectations and goals to come together as a global software development team.

However, despite this optimistic setting, I have found that virtual projects do not just happen. I have seen managers struggle with pressures unique to this type of environment. I have seen capable managers overlook integration aspects that have doomed a virtual project. These aspects have often had nothing to do with the technical nature of the project. They involve the delicate tasks of managing diverse cultural expectations, setting up responsibilities and a system of accountability, and of defining process and product ownership. These tasks are in addition to subtle changes in the usual cost, schedule, and quality issues that face all managers attempting to deliver products to a customer.

Why this Book?

Like many authors of management texts, my motivation for writing this book was to provide the software development community with a tool I wished I had had many times. My hope is that you will be able to avoid some of my mistakes. Virtual product development is considerably more complex than even the most complex project managed entirely in house. Moreover, circumstances may force a company into managing complex software development activities in a virtual environment. Such companies are often unprepared and have few resources to get them up to speed on this approach. Being the developer of a global product means using corporate resources from wherever you can find them. It means new opportunities, such as exploring the potential of using outside knowledge, lowering development costs, shortening schedules, achieving higher quality, and accessing markets that were heretofore unavailable. I have found virtual product development an exciting choice. It is a fast track to expanding choices and options, which can lead to a more competitive market edge and a more flexible and responsive software organization.

Although the main title suggests global development, the topics in this book apply to most distributed software development environments, even those across town. This book is intended to be an introduction to the many facets that involve managing software development in a diverse distributed environment.

What You Will Find

The text roughly follows the familiar software development life cycle. It begins with a look at the forces that have shaped the need for global software development and the foundations of this development strategy. It continues through the development life cycle, describing the necessary first steps to set up the development environment and project team. One of the first activities—and one commonly delayed too far into the project—is to effectively manage intellectual property. To aid those unfamiliar with this activity, the book includes a brief tutorial as an appendix. The type of business arrangement and contract can also greatly affect the project's outcome.

The book progresses through development, emphasizing the differences between traditional (management of a solely in-house project) and virtual management. The communication infrastructure is a critical aspect of virtual development. Software configuration management also takes on new importance, as do responsibility and accountability in general. The book devotes an entire chapter to maintenance, a stage that can pose problems, such as who is responsible for fixing what, if not planned early on. To aid managers in seeing life-cycle activities at a glance, the book includes a milestone chart and a brief description of the activity, including a cross reference to pertinent chapters (Appendix B).

The final chapter is perhaps the most important because it presents three case studies that illustrate the principles and activities described in the preceding chapters. For each study, I analyze choices made and offer a critical look at why certain aspects of the project contributed to its success—or failure.

I conclude the book with an epilogue that looks at the future of virtual management. I included this to stress that managers must be constantly aware of new developments and adjust their methods and practices accordingly. The techniques and methods presented here will continue to evolve as global telecommuting becomes more prevalent and the software development engineering community matures in their processes, tools, and management practices.

In all these chapters, my goal is to make it easy for managers to understand just what they must consider to manage a virtual project. Each chapter has a summary of key thoughts and the comprehensive index is designed to make it easy to quickly find the topic of interest. My aim is not to give a comprehensive tutorial on software project management. Indeed, I assume that most readers will have some background in software management practices and tools. I also do not provide a comprehensive treatment of individual topics, except intellectual property. There are many pointers to additional material for those who want to read more on a particular topic. The book is intended as a broad spectrum of information that will deepen the understanding of global software development.

As the software community intensifies its interest in virtual development, my hope is that the experiences and knowledge in this book will benefit those who want to take that first step toward a global development environment. Such a step could very well mean the difference between increased market share and a failing company, since software in the near future is likely to be designed for, maintained, and sold in the global market.

1

What's Driving Global Development?

If you're reading this book, you're probably at least mildly interested in global software development. You may have some notion about it and be wondering if it applies to your organization. You may be anxious, having heard some claims of spectacular successes and some rumors of spectacular failures. You may believe you can avoid it altogether. You may have even asked one of these questions when debating the usefulness of global software development:

- Can't we just work harder and get better tools to lower the high costs of developing software in house?

- Won't that 200K of legacy Cobol running the company's accounting department be around for another 10 years?

- Why do we need to learn another language? Isn't English always the universal business language?

- Won't a product marketed overseas sell just as well as it has in the US?

- Can't the staff use e-mail to coordinate this cutting edge project and be just as successful not working with the guys across town, on the other coast, or in another country?

All these questions have one thing in common. The answer to each is a resounding "no."

For better or worse, times have changed, and so has a large part of software development "tradition." To keep their market edge, organizations cannot rely on the same software-engineering management skills they use for in-house development. Managers must update their skills in managing people, workflow, and technology.

Industry Drivers

Why is this trend emerging? One reason is that the software-development industry itself is changing.

Supply and Demand

The demand for software services has historically outpaced the supply of people who perform them. As microcomputers and controllers proliferate, the demand for software continues to increase at a faster pace than the supply, as Figure 1.1 shows.

Until the early 1980s, approximately 75 to 80 percent of the world's software was being produced in the US, and most of the supply was met with people who lived there [1, 2]. By the mid-1990s, however, the need for these professionals had increased to the point at which there were not enough resources to meet it. Labor costs escalated as companies competed for resources. As equivalent resources became available at a lower cost—especially overseas—work started to migrate outside the company. In essence, the supply and demand of software professionals was driving costs, which in turn was driving the migration of software development outside company walls. Today, many companies are finding it economically attractive to outsource or codevelop software overseas. The current market for outsourcing software outside the US is estimated between $200 million and $50 billion [3, 4, 5] and it is still growing.

Global Market

Another industry driver is the shift from a predominantly US to a global market. Although the US is still the largest software manufacturer (and yes, software is becoming "manufactured" as the industry matures), the global market is estimated to be more than $120 billion [6]. Microsoft, for example, derived 55 percent of its sales from outside the US [1]. Other

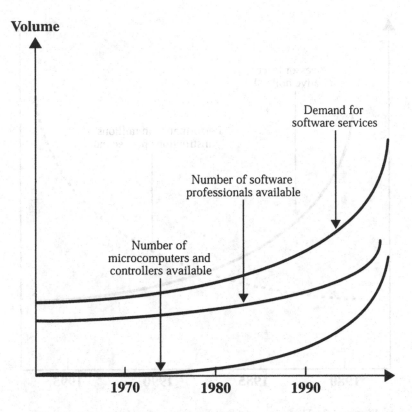

Volume

Demand for
software services

Number of software
professionals available

Number of
microcomputers and
controllers available

1970   1980   1990

Figure 1.1: The demand for software professionals in relation to microcom-
puter/controller proliferation.

software producers, on average, derive 58 percent of their sales from outside the US [7].

Moreover, the market for software development and products will increase faster outside the US than within the US. The reason is the increase
in price-performance ratios of computers, a trend shown in Figure 1.2.

Computers, especially lower end types like PCs, are less expensive,
contain more computing power, and include more features and functions
than they did even one year ago. There has been a proliferation of these less
expensive, more powerful computers, and the rest of the world is catching
up to the explosion in US computer sales over the last decade. The electronics industry as a whole has seen this trend in televisions and VCRs,

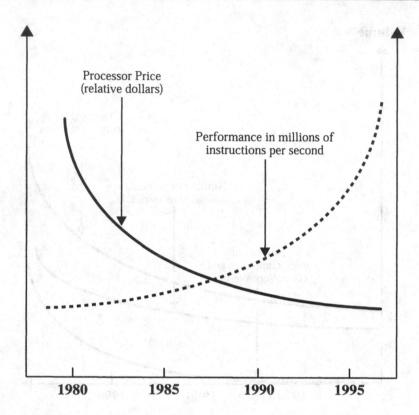

Figure 1.2: The price-performance ratio of computers over time.

for example. However, unlike its predecessors, computer hardware can be upgraded piecemeal and software is upwardly compatible with the new hardware. This characteristic plus the ability to load multiple programs on a machine is making software development a very competitive and profitable business. For those who produce software, this means they can no longer pass off a product with poor quality or average performance. It is no longer a seller's market. Customers will start demanding software that meets more of their particular needs, as Figure 1.3 shows.

Indeed, in the US, the industry has already seen this trend realized in software packages such as word processors, spreadsheets, and computer-aided design packages: the software has experienced a market shakeout driven by price and how the products met customer needs.

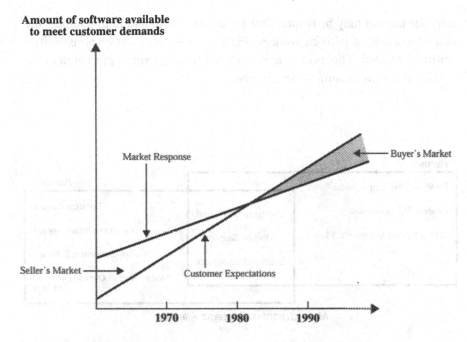

Figure 1.3: Demands for software as the market matures.

Business Drivers

Global software development is also occurring because of certain business arrangements, such as strategic partnerships and joint ventures. It may also be required because your company is already competing in a global market.

Strategic Partnerships

Companies are relying more on strategic partnerships to develop and promote their software products—generally to gain market access. In these situations, a product may exist but needs market channels through an established vendor in the new market.

A strategic partnership, or alliance, may require that an existing product be modified or supported by companies other than the one that developed it. Often, interfaces between customers and feedback on how the software meets customer needs are divided among the partners. Occasionally, one partner may be responsible for development and maintenance; the other for working with customers. Figure 1.4 shows how responsibilities could be divided. The more shared responsibilities (overlapping area in the figure), the more complex the alliance.

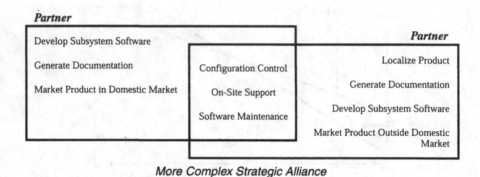

More Complex Strategic Alliance

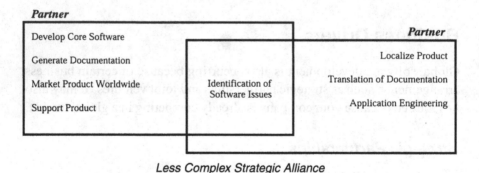

Less Complex Strategic Alliance

Figure 1.4: Two possible divisions of responsibility in a strategic partnership.

Given the depth of responsibilities in the partner companies and the importance of software to products and business operations, it is almost inevitable that companies will deal with some aspects of global software development.

Joint Ventures

Most joint ventures result in a separate company being formed that has
fiscal responsibilities to the joint venture partners. Figure 1.5 shows this
relationship. The establishment of a separate entity is the main difference
between a strategic partnership and a joint venture.

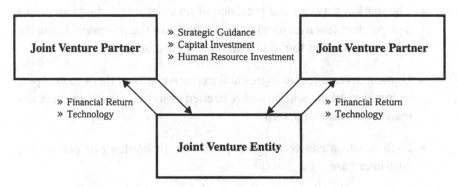

Figure 1.5: Major expectations of a joint venture relationship.

How much of the joint venture each partner owns determines its influence and activities. One partner may bring working and equipment capital,
while the other provides technical resources. One partner may bring expertise in one type of technology, such as graphical user interfaces, while the
other brings another technology, such as database management.

Joint ventures may be legislated by the country in which the partners
want to do business. They tend to have more financial pressure to succeed
and thus more frequently aim to develop software at the lowest cost. This
makes them more open to the global development option.

Global Companies

Your company may already be performing business on a global scale. If so,
global software development may be a joint product development between
two divisions, the same division in different locations, or two companies
under the parent holding company.

Some global companies treat subsidiaries as isolated profit centers—
the success of that company or division is measured in terms of how much

profit it returns to headquarters. This tends to inhibit joint efforts between companies or divisions if the risks and costs are higher than for in-house developments or a short-term return isn't projected or demonstrated.

Recently, more global companies have opted to synergize their diverse capital and human assets. There are several advantages to this:

- The market network and presence of an existing product can help a new product (even an unrelated one) because the personnel know the customers and are familiar with the support facilities.

- Uniting diverse technologies and expertise allows them to compete in larger markets and provides needed resources that can meet demand at a reasonable cost.

- Each location can focus on a particular technology or part of the customer base.

- They can merge divisions or companies and still keep separate locations.

- They can acquire other companies and their products and technologies to complement their business strategy.

- They can migrate or establish a technology center at a different geographic location.

What Will Change?

As these global development drivers show, software development managers are facing more complex environments—strategic partnerships, joint ventures, joint development with other divisions within a global company—each with its own set of needs that require unique methods of organization and control. In-house environments are also changing.

In each of these scenarios, except in-house development, software is produced in geographically dispersed locations. In all cases, the common thread is the virtual software development team. In the next chapter, I describe the characteristics of that team.

Strategic Partnerships

Strategic partnerships usually don't require a large capital investment (such as purchasing the same software development tools), but require more integration of structures and practices. This means blending sets of management practices, development practices, tools, and configuration management systems. Even with secrecy or nondisclosure agreements in place, however, partners may be reluctant to share technology. Management must be able to recognize this environment and work effectively within it.

Joint Ventures

Joint ventures, on the other hand, involve a unique entity, so less blending is required. However, there will be some cultural adjustments—everyone must understand what the parent companies bring to and expect from, the new company. Technology innovations and sharing are also more straightforward.

Global Companies

Global companies already have diverse management philosophies, software development practices, tools, and so on, among their divisions. Joint software development management skills must be applied to overcome these differences, and if divisions are in different countries, to overcome cultural differences. Technology sharing issues are usually dealt with at the corporate level.

In-House Developments

In-house development, always an option for software projects, will continue to evolve to meet the company's business or product needs. As is true today, shared capital investment and technology will often be needed to make the project successful. Organizations will need to keep pace with the rate of technology change to remain competitive.

Key Thoughts

Global software development is inevitable because of both industry drivers, such as the supply and demand of technical resources and the increasingly global software market, and business arrangements, such as strategic partnerships, joint ventures, and global companies.

Each of these has its own focus for joint development, but all require new skills in information transfer, adjusting to cultural and philosophical differences, and technology sharing. All require managing a virtual software development team.

Bibliography

[1] C.L. Miller, "Transborder Tips and Traps," *Byte*, Vol. 19, No. 6, June 1994, p. 93.

[2] G. Bission, "Firms Expanding Abroad Face Culture, Sticker Shock," *MacWeek*, Vol. 7, No. 24, June 14, 1993, pp. 38–41.

[3] T. Krepchin, "When Offshore Programming Works," *Datamation*, Vol. 39, No. 14, July 15, 1993, pp. 55–56.

[4] T.L. Speer, "Programming Ships Out to Cheaper Climates," *Corporate Computing*, Vol. 1, No. 3, Sept. 1992, p. 21.

[5] J.R. Patane and J. Jurison, "Is Global Outsourcing Diminishing the Prospects for American Programmers?" *J. Systems Management*, Vol. 45, No. 6, June 1994, pp. 6–10.

[6] J. Markoff, "U.S. Lead in Software Faces a Rising Threat," *New York Times*, Vol. 142, Sunday ed., Oct. 25, 1992, Col. 1, p. E16.

[7] Y. Malhotra, "Controlling Copyright Infringements of Intellectual Property: The Case of Computer Software—Part One," *J. Systems Management*, Vol. 45, No. 6, June 1994, p. 32.

2

Introducing the Virtual Software Organization

A joint software development project—whether with another company or another division in the same company—must be managed and controlled. The people must be motivated, the resources allocated, and the product quality protected. That is, the goals are the same as if you had everyone in one spot, but the way you achieve those goals is decidedly different. To see why, you must first understand the characteristics of the virtual software organization.

Virtual vs. Nonvirtual

Like anything virtual, an entity behaves as if it exists physically, but it has no physical form. A virtual organization still has people, assigned activities, communication paths, workplaces, and other items familiar to a centrally located, or nonvirtual, work organization. The obvious difference between the two organizations is that, in a virtual organization, parts of the project are not colocated but behave as if they are. Another major difference is that the virtual organization exists solely to produce something—software, hardware, documentation, or customer support. It derives its definition from a particular development effort. The nonvirtual organization can also exist to produce something, but it is also defined by business objectives and so may exist outside a particular project.

In a loose interpretation, virtual organizations are not new. A sales department is an example. In many companies, sales people spend much time visiting the customer's location and so do not interact with the rest of the organization in real-time. That is, communications are physically distributed between the organization and the customer site. Individual sales people also work together to provide services. However—and this is where the similarity to a true virtual organization (such as a software development team) breaks down—sales people typically do not depend heavily on other members of the sales organization to provide a service.

A better example of a virtual relationship is the close interaction between customer representatives and a supplier, such as that found in software beta testing. The two are in different locations but are working together to solve a problem. Here, team members depend more heavily on each other to produce a product or provide services.

Figure 2.1 shows how a virtual and a nonvirtual development project contrast. In the alpha project, the team conducts all activities within the same physical proximity. Interactions are between physical beings interfacing at the same moment. In the beta software project, the team members are not colocated, so communications may not exist at the same moment; meetings, the exchange of ideas, and results are done independently among various members.

Do I Need a Virtual Project Team?

How do you know when the project should be virtual? A virtual software development organization can take many forms. Members of a single team can work at home or at different office locations. Separate software teams can develop different parts of a product in different locations or the development team can be in one location and the maintenance team in another. In many cases, your virtual organization will involve outsourcing—using outside software development resources for part of your software project, whether that is another company or a different part of your own company. To see whether you need to outsource ask yourself the following questions:

Do business arrangements dictate it? Your company's business arrangements may have changed because of a joint venture, strategic partnership, merger, acquisition, or other business reason. In this case the question of whether to outsource has been decided.

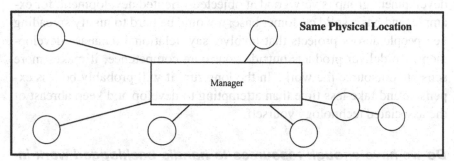

Alpha Project – Nonvirtual

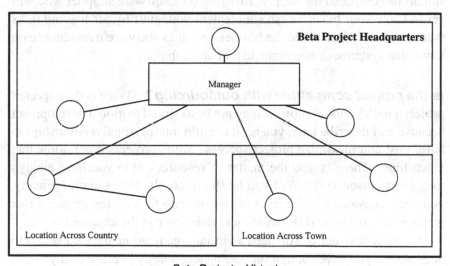

Beta Project – Virtual

Figure 2.1: Nonvirtual versus a virtual project structure.

Do we want to emphasize our core competencies?   Companies have recently begun emphasizing a business strategy that involves concentrating on core technical or business competencies. If your company or development group is very good at objected-oriented development, for example, and has a solid customer base, it would be hard to justify spreading key people across projects that involve, say, relational database development. To deliver products outside your core competence, it makes more sense to outsource the work. In the long run, it will probably be less expensive and take less time than attempting to develop and keep abreast of the associated technology yourself.

Do we have enough resources to handle backlogged work internally?   This is probably the most frequently occurring reason for outsourcing work. As I describe in Chapter 1, the demand for software professionals has outpaced the supply. Bringing on a software supplier who will get to know your business can supplement your staff by off-loading tasks that are not as important to the business, such as software maintenance on low-value systems, or nonstrategic tool development.

Is the project compatible with outsourcing?   What is the expected project length? Shorter projects may not be as suited to global development because, as I describe later, you need to build interpersonal relationships to build trust and maximize project success. Some projects don't allow that much time. There is also the matter of resources. Do you have enough to support outsourcing? Will you be sharing tools, for example? Finally, you need to evaluate if the risks of outsourcing fit with the project's risk management strategy. (I describe these risks later in the chapter.)

If you decide that you do need a virtual organization, the next step is to determine if you have enough supporting technology in place or if you can add it cost-effectively.

Virtual Technology

Virtual organizations have evolved largely because of technology improvements over the last decade. These include improved communications structure, increased communication bandwidth, decreased communication cost, better price-performance ratio for microcomputers and controllers, and better software. Technology has made it easier and more cost-effective to manage organizations that are not colocated. I describe communications technology and methods in more detail in Chapter 6.

A virtual organization must be able first to communicate in a distributed fashion and second to communicate effectively along the spectrum from real time to non-real time. As Figure 2.2 shows, technology has made the second goal more feasible; communication has always existed in a distributed manner, but until lately it was not deemed very effective. Voice mail, faxes, electronic mail, bulletin boards, databases, pagers, portable telephones, and so on, have increased our ability to communicate meaningfully. Cellular telephones, videoconferencing, and pagers have allowed access to instant information, thus increasing information frequency. Access to stored information through voice mail, e-mail, and bulletin boards has increased information bandwidth.

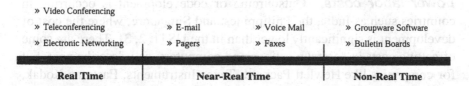

Figure 2.2: Classification of virtual technology according to real-time, near-real time, and non-real-time delivery.

Virtual technology includes the use of video and telephone conferencing, pagers, and electronic "chat" capabilities for real- and near-real-time communications. For non-real-time communication, the technology includes voice and e-mail, bulletin boards, and databases that contain common project information, such as schedules, problems, and the shared software and tools in groupware packages. Some or all of these technologies must be in place for a virtual software development project to be successful.

Benefits

The organizations that first benefited from the technology improvements were those most comfortable with new technology and change—in most cases, those that dealt with computers, software, and communications. These types of organizations will be the first to benefit from the concepts and technology associated with the virtual organization as well. Depending on the virtual organization's structure and function, companies can look forward to:

Lower overhead (fixed) costs.   The members of the organization can perform their functions at a location that costs less to operate (smaller office space) or possibly nothing to operate (working at home). Software production takes a far lower capital investment relative to other industries that demand large tooling and production space.

Lower labor costs.   Outsourcing or codevelopment is occurring in countries such as India, the Philippines, and Singapore, where the cost of development is significantly lower than in the US [1, 2, 3]. There are some offsetting costs in communications and computers, as I describe next, but for companies like Hewlett Packard, Texas Instruments, Eastman Kodak, Continental Bank, General Dynamics, Time Warner, and Sun Microsystems, these investment costs are insignificant compared to the labor cost saved.

Increased morale.   Employees in the virtual organization may be independent enough to feel comfortable working at home (telecommuting) or working on the road using virtual technology to help produce a product or provide services. As virtual technology becomes more commonplace, and companies begin to consider the individual work preferences of talented employees, this mode of working can have a positive effect on those able to use it. Current research is exploring personality traits that are suitable for virtual teams that work away from the office [4].

More flexibility and project options. This is particularly true when work is divided across time zones. At first, this may seem to decrease visibility and control, but as software organizations have experienced, the development of a software product goes beyond an eight-hour day [5, 6]. A good manager can wrap up development in Europe; feed the results to the development team in California; and at the end of their day, feed the results back to the European team, who are fresh and ready to make additional progress. Current research is exploring how virtual organizations are transforming management science [7].

Risks

Of course, going virtual is not without risk. Most, if not all, of these risks depend on the quality of project management. Once they are addressed, almost any company can build an effective virtual organization.

Decreased morale. If your organization is not comfortable with the technology and working more independently, the morale of the team, and possibly of the organization, will suffer. If the organization is not prepared or managed properly for this type of work environment, morale will also suffer. Look at lessons from past efforts in which the company introduced similar technology to guide your expectations.

Loss of face-to-face. No matter how good your video equipment is, how clear your communications lines are, or how often you electronically mail or fax information, the loss of face-to-face communication will evoke feelings of disconnection. The workplace is a social gathering. As Jack Patterson observes, a virtual workplace will weaken and break the traditional bonds between employers and employees, and among employees themselves [8]. Understanding people's motives, agendas, and other human interactions in the workplace will be more difficult in the virtual organization. There will be no body language, facial expressions, and other forms of nonverbal communication. This limited interaction will occur daily. Team members' competence, honesty, and reliability must be taken on faith. For example, in one project I know, a team from Japan was working with a team from the US. They used e-mail and phone calls almost exclusively, with occasional video conferencing. The project reports indicated no problem and e-mail was cordial. However, when the two teams began joint design reviews at each other's location, they discovered a major lack of progress. The US team was dismayed. They had repeatedly asked if there was any difficulty and been assured that everything was progressing without problems. As it turned out, the Japanese team had faced tough technical issues and was having difficulty getting through them. Had there been a face-to-face meeting, the body language of the Japanese would have prompted the US team to inquire more deeply about the reports. They might also have probed more deeply had they understood that Japanese culture pretty much requires a consensus on difficult issues.

Lack of trust.　　Lack of trust is a natural consequence of losing face-to-face interaction. Indeed, trust in the virtual organization has been explored from both a legal and management viewpoint. From a legal viewpoint, the privacy and security of information must be maintained and audited to ensure that a proper culture exists for an organization's employees and customers, yet such activities are done by people who have no direct contact with the organization's day-to-day operations (virtual workers). As Robert Posch suggests, organizations should consider activities such as a fair information practices audit, a record retention program, and a constant legal review when reviewing legal trust issues within the virtual organization and with customers [9].

From a management viewpoint, trust must be earned. For the virtual organization, Charles Handy lists seven rules of trust that management must constantly address [10]:

- *Trust is not blind.* Trust must come in smaller groups within the organization to build trust in the larger organization.

- *Trust needs boundaries.* There must be freedom to perform work within boundaries of control.

- *Trust demands learning.* Groups must be flexible enough to change when times and customers demand it and must be able to keep themselves abreast of change.

- *Trust must be tough.* When trust is misplaced, the people who misplaced the trust must go.

- *Trust needs bonding.* Personal statements and examples from the organization's leaders build trust in the organization.

- *Trust needs touch.* The more virtual the organization, the more people need to meet in person. This does not mean daily, of course, but there should be some plan to have the team members meet regularly, say, every other month or at least quarterly in a year-long project.

- *Trust requires leaders.* Not just one leader, but many. Different leaders play different roles, cementing trust within the organization with their different perspectives. When leaders with different perspectives trust each other in a virtual organization, they become role models for the rest of the team.

Costs

Without a proper infrastructure, the cost of setting up and maintaining a virtual organization is not small. Part of the decision-making process is weighing benefits against costs. The following are the major costs associated with virtual organizations:

- *Additional capital investment.* This includes one time costs like additional computer equipment, upgrades, and supplies. The team will need high-speed modems and access to high-speed communication lines either through a LAN or Internet service provider. You are also likely to need additional phone lines, a voice messaging system, and video equipment.

- *Additional operating costs.* These costs are typically smaller, but you will incur them throughout the project. They include added long-distance telephone charges and communication lease time (such as through an ISP) and higher travel expenses.

- *Additional administrative and project costs.* These include groupware and software upgrades to enhance cooperative work, additional software development tools, the extra overhead associated with expanding configuration management practices, and the cost of personnel to maintain communication services.

For most organizations, these items are already part of their infrastructure for local software development and communications needs, so the incremental cost of supporting a virtual organization is not usually overwhelming. The difference is the price of communications and control to support an organization that is not local.

Putting a Virtual Team Together

Assuming you have the required virtual technology, the benefits outweigh the risks, and the cost is acceptable, the next step is to pull the team together. One of the first issues you may have to consider is the language the team will use. Although English is frequently considered the universal business language, there are exceptions to its use. If the customer does business in another language, the supplier is typically expected to use that language. This is common in countries like Japan, France, and Italy.

Another issue to consider is the comfort and cooperation level of individual team members. Try to put the virtual team members together for a time before the project so that they can get to know each other and build relationships. For example, in one project, two geographically distant divisions—one in Louisiana and one in California—met for a week in Colorado to work on informal team building exercises and just to get to know each other. Because the location was neutral to both teams, they began on an equal footing and many were able to form strong individual relationships that lasted throughout the project. This team building duration is fairly typical. Some case studies recommend as long as six to 18 months for team building if the project can allow it [11, 12].

	Software Development Life-Cycle Phase				
	Pre-Development	Requirements	Design	Code	Test
Identify need for a virtual team	XXX				
Apply virtual technology	XXX	XXX	XXX	XXX	XXX
Manage risks	XXX	XXX	XXX	XXX	XXX
Pull the team together	XXX	XXX			

Table 2.1: Applying the steps in creating a virtual organization to software development.

Going Virtual in the Development Life Cycle

So far, I have identified four main issues in establishing a virtual organization. Table 2.1 shows how these fit into a typical software development life-cycle. Appendix B of this book gives a more detailed milestone chart.

As the table shows, it is best to identify the need for a virtual team before the project starts. You can go virtual after the team has formed and has entered the requirements phase, but any later than that will interrupt established lines of communication, which is likely to impact the team's productivity. In one project, a US company decided to outsource part of the software they were attempting to develop completely internally. Their reasoning was that outsourcing would dramatically lower costs, which were getting out of hand. Unfortunately, they were driven to choose the lowest bidder, a company in India. The decision was a bad one. The US team had to spend many hours away from work on the other parts of the software to bring the new team up to speed and monitor their progress. They essentially had to build a virtual infrastructure on the fly. The project not only lost money but the product was even later to the customer than expected with internal development alone. This is a clear case of not thinking through the demands of a virtual team.

You must apply virtual technology before or when the project starts and continue it until the project ends. You should establish and test-run software such as groupware, bulletin boards, and electronic mail before large-scale use. In later phases, you can add virtual technology as needed to facilitate communications and information sharing.

You must also assess the risk of implementing virtual organizations before the project starts and continue until the project ends. Issues to assess include trust, communications, and other human aspects, along with costs and benefits.

Finally, you should identify your team, or at least your leaders, no later than the requirements phase. If you do this much later, the team's communication and hence efficiency will suffer.

Another important issue I've not yet mentioned is project documentation. In a virtual project, documentation is the glue that holds the project together—more so than in nonvirtual projects. Documentation such as the software development plan outlines roles and responsibilities. Requirements specifications and plans such as quality assurance identify expectations for all team members before issues come up and cause confusion. The reference to, maintenance, and ownership of these documents and the benefits they provide are critical in large teams with geographically dispersed members.

Key Thoughts

A virtual organization is decentralized and exists to produce products or services. This contrasts to a nonvirtual organization in which all interaction is done in a single location and the entity exists apart from a particular project. Before forming a virtual team, you must first identify a need and have access to virtual technology such as video and telephone conferencing, pagers, and electronic chat capabilities, as well as to databases and other groupware. You must also be reasonably certain that the benefits outweigh the risks. Benefits include improved costs, possible morale improvements, and management flexibility. Risks include decreased morale, lack of face-to-face contact, and lack of trust.

The cost of implementing a virtual team is lower if your organization has the required technology in place to support in-house projects. It is best to identify the need for a virtual team before the project starts. Apply virtual technology before or when the project starts and continue it until the project ends. Establish and test-run software such as groupware, bulletin boards, and electronic mail before large-scale use. Also assess the risk of implementing virtual organizations before the project starts and continue until the project ends. Look at human aspects, such as trust, as well as costs and benefits. Documentation is the glue that holds a virtual project together, because it defines responsibilities and sets expectations.

Bibliography

[1] L. MacDonald, "Software Concerns Thrive in Philippines—Cheap Labor Makes Data-Input Firms Big Exporters," *Wall Street J.*, Friday ed., May 10, 1991, pp. B4B–B3A.

[2] T. Gandy, "Switch on to India," *Banker*, Vol. 145, No. 832, June 1995, pp. 74–76.

[3] E. Yourdon, "Developing Software Overseas," *Byte*, Vol. 19, No. 6, June, 1994, pp. 113–120.

[4] M. Loverder, *The Effects of Individuals' Psychological Needs on Telecommuting's Impact on Job Performance*, Ph.D. Dissertation, Illinois Institute of Technology, 1997.

[5] D.H. Freedman, "Culture of Urgency," *Forbes ASAP*, Sept. 12, 1993, pp. 25–28.

[6] R.L. Scheire, "US Firms Save Costs by Tapping Programming Talent Overseas," *PC Week*, Vol. 12., No. 13, Apr. 3, 1995, pp. E1–E3.

[7] C. Faucheux, "How Virtual Organizing is Transforming Management Science," *Comm. ACM*, Vol. 40, No. 9., Sept. 1997, pp. 50–55.

[8] J. Patterson, "Welcome to the Company That Isn't There," *Business Week*, Oct. 17, 1994, pp. 86–88.

[9] R. Posch, "Maintaining Public Trust in the Virtual Organization World," *Direct Marketing*, Vol. 57, May 1994, pp. 76–79.

[10] C. Handy, "Trust and the Virtual Organization," *Harvard Business Review*, Vol. 73, May–June 1995, pp. 40–50.

[11] B. Geber, "Virtual Teams," *Training*, Vol. 34, No. 4, Apr. 1995, pp. 36–40.

[12] E. Harding, "US Companies Finding that CASE Travels Well in India—Surplus of Skilled Software Professionals Makes Outsourcing, Joint Projects Attractive," *Software Magazine*, Vol. 11, No. 14, Nov. 15, 1991, pp. 24–28.

3
First Steps

Assuming you have established a need to outsource at least some of the product, have the required technology, and have determined that the cost-benefit ratio and risks are acceptable, what do you do now? The first steps should be to lay a solid foundation for global development and unite everyone's expectations about lines of responsibility, schedules, cost, and other business and technical concerns. The most straightforward way to do this is through a contract when you are outsourcing outside the company and through a requirements specification and project schedule when you are outsourcing to another part of your company.

Elements of a Good Contract

You must consider several contract items when you outsource or subcontract part of your software development project to another company. I've seen projects lose money or even fail because management failed to specify details such as the version of tools to be used or the type of tests the outsourced work must pass. The outsourcing failed to meet expectations because these issues weren't addressed through a statement of work early in the project.

Statement of Work

A statement of work identifies what must be performed or delivered and over what timeframe. Because it is a legal document, it should be as unambiguous as possible.

A good SOW should describe:

- *Tasks or activities to be performed.* This is the main part of the SOW. The text should communicate the expectations and limits of the work in a form the supplier understands.

- *Deliverables.* These include software source code, documentation, and tools to be used. This is important in evaluating results because it identifies the products that will help close out the supplier's efforts.

- *Where the tasks or activities are to be performed.* Sometimes the work is expected to be done at a certain location. By identifying these expectations in the SOW, the contract lets the supplier plan and cost the effort accurately.

- *Standards or methods to be followed.* If you are outsourcing part of the software project to be integrated later or plan to maintain the outsourced software, the development or design methods, style, and documentation should closely resemble what your organization is used to.

- *Timeframe or schedule for tasks and deliverables.* This might be only a list of dates, but it helps bound the effort and communicate critical expectations. By understanding tasks and deliverables in terms of a schedule, the supplier will be in a better position to estimate the resources needed.

- *Communications/status methods and meetings.* Expectations of how the supplier's activities are to be monitored and how communications between the customer and supplier are to be handled are often overlooked. Spelling out methods for monitoring and communication is especially important when the customers and supplier are located more than three time zones from each other.

- *Type of equipment to be used.* Identifying the development platforms, target platforms, test tools, and other related equipment helps ensure that the software will execute and test properly in its intended environment.

- *Special interface and performance requirements.* If the software has to integrate into other software, or fit with specialized hardware, the SOW should identify interface, performance, timing, and other similar requirements. It should also refer to industry standards or any special interface documents.

- *Miscellaneous items.* These include items such as the programming language and target hardware dependencies that are unique to your product, business, or development process.

In addition to this list, the SOW should set expectations for the type of business relationship you want to pursue with an outsourced supplier. It identifies the degree of freedom the supplier and customer expect.

Cost Structures

Those you contract to do outsourcing are typically motivated by economic gain, not by the technical and marketing goals of your project. The cost structure you select can greatly influence both your profit margin and that of the organization you contract. Figure 3.1 shows the range of cost structure types. The two most popular—fixed price and cost plus—are at opposite ends of the spectrum. The type of cost structure you choose is based mainly on the financial risk you and your supplier are willing to accept and on the potential financial reward.

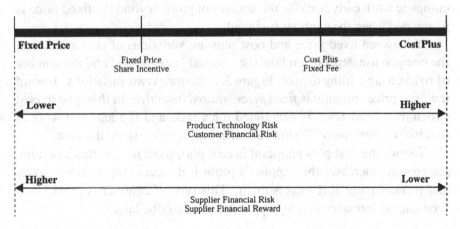

Figure 3.1: Cost structures in terms of risk

As the figure shows, a *fixed price* cost structure is the least risky for the company outsourcing the work (customer). In this type of contract, the services and deliverables identified in the SOW are bid at a particular amount that cannot be exceeded. If the supplier expends more than originally bid and agreed to, it assumes the extra financial burden to complete the tasks. Likewise, if the supplier spends less than originally bid, it keeps the difference as additional profit.

Usually, fixed price contracts are considered very conservative for software development because they represent a low product technology risk. They also typically have a higher estimated price because suppliers try to mitigate financial risks by padding the cost to one higher than normally expected.

At the other extreme are *cost plus* contracts. These are structured so that the company outsourcing the work assumes most of the financial risk. The services and deliverables are based on a negotiated price plus reimbursement of additional cost if needed to complete the tasks specified in the SOW. Cost plus contracts are usually proposed when the product technology risk is high.

In this cost structure, the additional financial risk is charged back and reimbursed by the customer. From the supplier perspective, there is no risk of financial loss on work performed. There is also no financial incentive to complete work early because the amount of profit beyond the fixed price is negotiated when the contract is signed.

In between fixed price and cost plus are variations of cost structures; the one you use depends on how the contract is negotiated and the amount of risk you are willing to take. Figure 3.1 illustrates two variations. Toward the fixed price endpoint is *fixed price, shared incentive*. In this type of cost structure, a fixed price is negotiated for a task, and if additional work is required to meet the SOW, the customer and supplier share the cost.

Toward the cost plus endpoint is *cost plus, fixed fee*. In this structure, the contract increases the supplier's profit if it meets program milestones and reduces profit if it misses them. This type of contract is good when schedule performance is a high priority, as I describe later.

Investment Capital and Capital Equipment

As part of outsourcing, an organization must decide to what degree it will allow the supplier access to investment capital and capital equipment. Pertinent questions here are

- *Is access to certain types of equipment necessary to perform the tasks?* In many cases, the supplier needs access to capital equipment to perform the work. For example, if the supplier is to develop parts of software for customized hardware, it must access that hardware for testing.

- *Is the relationship short-term or long-term?* If the relationship is short term and involves only one project, access may not be needed. On the other hand, a strategic partnership or joint venture that involves codevelopment or access to markets will typically demand a large capital investment.

- *What is the payback or benefit?* The answer depends on the financial investment and risk you want to assume. Is the amount of required investment greater than the potential return? What are the opportunity costs and benefits? Financial investment should be only one consideration.

- *Is ownership of patents/technology tied to capital and equipment access?* If capital investment and equipment access results in technology innovation, how will it be protected? Who will have ownership? Who will benefit? Do not ignore issues involving the ownership of intellectual property rights. For those unfamiliar with mechanisms for intellectual property protection, I present a brief tutorial in Appendix A of this book.

These are just four considerations; others will come up, depending on your motivation for outsourcing, your relationship with the supplier, and other business agreements.

Warranty

Most commercial software today—either sold as is or integrated into a product—has explicit or implied warranties. You can view a warranty from two perspectives, either separately or together, depending on the nature of your business and how software integrates into the product.

- *Warranty of the software delivered to your customers.* Here, you must address how the outsourced software will be included in the product's warranty. Typically, the warranty of the entire software product supersedes any warranties from the outsourced supplier.

- *Warranty of the software you receive from the supplier.* Here, you must concern yourself with structuring some warranty agreement with the supplier.

The second view of warranty is more subtle, but its omission can spell disaster. Suppose you delivered software with a bug to many customers. Suppose also that the bug means you must issue an upgrade to fix a possible data corruption, or it results in a lawsuit against your company. After investigating, you find that the bug can be isolated to software you outsourced.

Now what? If the warranty agreement does not spell out certain issues, questions remain unanswered: Will the supplier reimburse you for costs associated with warranty claims? Did the supplier have to meet some sort of acceptance criteria or test as part of the warranty condition? Were time limits associated with explicit or implied warranties?

As you can see, a warranty involves many issues, which depend on the particular development. I can't possibly identify them all here. My objective is to point out that you must consider warranty issues as part of outsourcing, especially if you plan to integrate the software into a product associated with major financial or safety issues.

Schedule and Performance

Most companies that provide outsourcing are motivated by profit. Unfortunately, these profit motives sometimes conflict with schedule and performance expectations.

In a cost plus contract, for example, the supplier may be content to stretch the job as long as it can knowing that the cost for performing the work is covered plus a negotiated profit. In this case the supplier's profit margin may be higher than that of the customer integrating the supplier's software—a customer that may be on a fixed price contract. Thus motivations for completing the job conflict.

Payments and incentives should be based on meeting schedule milestones and technical performance criteria, as Figure 3.2 shows. In this example, payments to the supplier are tied to the acceptance of deliverables, such as requirements specifications, design documents, and test plans. The division of payments, shown as a percentage of the total cost, are weighted evenly except the last one—the one associated with closing out open items after delivery. You should vary the weight associated with the division of payments to emphasize the relative importance of milestones during the schedule. For example, if certain milestones are on the project's critical path, those milestones should have a higher payment weight.

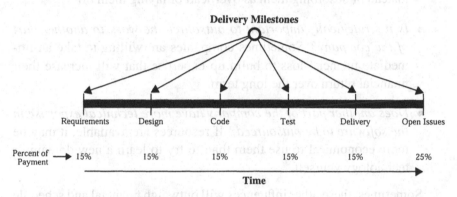

Figure 3.2: Supplier payments based on meeting milestone deliverables.

Outsourcing Within a Company

At first, this seems a contradiction in terms, but with many companies already globally based, it is not so far-fetched to contract part of the software to a different part of the company.

This type of outsourcing is different from outsourcing outside a company. The accounting and financial rules are different and decisions may be influenced more heavily by company policies and politics. This means making lines of ownership clear and establishing a staffing plan early on. You can typically take on more risk in this type of outsourcing because the "supplier" has more than profit as a motivation.

Many aspects are also the same for both types. For example, no matter where you outsource your project, you must have a statement of expectations, you must look at schedule and performance options, and you must continually review budgetary expectations to ensure that you achieve the desired return on investment.

However, outsourcing within a company requires addressing issues in addition to these:

- *Does one part of the company need the work?* Sometimes another group has a gap between projects and may need to cover their staff instead of absorbing them as overhead or laying them off.

- *Is it strategically important to outsource the work to another part of the company?* Sometimes companies are willing to take an immediate financial loss to build up expertise that will increase their financial return over the long term.

- *Does another part of the company have more technical expertise in the software to be outsourced?* If resources are available, it may be more economical to use them than to try to learn a new domain or technology yourself.

Sometimes, these other influences will outweigh financial and schedule concerns in your decision.

Ownership

Establishing ownership of the software should be done early in the process. By "ownership," I mean that the supplier must recognize its responsibility for the quality and integrity of the software, along with the development process and schedule.

One way to ensure ownership is to have the supplier take responsibility for the technical solution. For example, if the supplier's task is to understand software diagnostic routines, don't supply the algorithms on how to perform the diagnostics. If you dictate the technical solution, the supplier may not be as willing to deal with implementation problems down the road.

Another strategy for ensuring ownership is to help the supplier understand the broad picture and how its work applies. If you are working on a client-server application and are outsourcing part of the server software, educate your supplier by demonstrating how other subsystems use the data the supplier's software creates. By communicating your intent, not just handing the supplier a set of specifications, you can avoid many integration problems later on.

Many factors affect ownership that you cannot influence. Organization motivations, biases, and unwilling participants are just a few. Hopefully, with good leadership and perseverance, you can overcome these or at least soften their influence.

Staffing

Although staffing is somewhat of an issue when outsourcing outside your company, it is far more important when outsourcing within your company. Most organizations do not have enough people to cover existing projects, let alone new ones. To accommodate new work, companies must shift priorities or hire new people. Either way, this can slow progress if it is not properly planned.

As a first step, create a staffing plan and have upper management review it. It is vital that you get management's buy-in so that you receive the resources you need to meet your project schedule.

Commitment

Because an internal supplier is not motivated solely by profit, you must look at other sources for establishing a high commitment level.

Commitment is motivated both internally, within the group, and externally, from corporate policy. Internal motivations for working on outsourced software include the need for work, an interest in the project, a chance to expand the knowledge and understanding of a particular technology, and individual motivators such as a chance to travel or be exposed to a different part of the company. External motivations include the need for new business to meet quarterly or annual financial targets, directives from higher management, and the need to conform with corporate strategy.

Understanding the motivations behind commitment will help you resolve problems, such as staffing assignments and budgetary allocations.

Although you may be powerless over some factors, helping to influence the commitment to your software project will make it more successful.

Key Thoughts

A solid contract is the first step in any effort to outsource software outside your company. A contract should include a statement of work that covers such things as tasks, activities, monitoring mechanisms, and schedules. It should also specify the cost structure, access to investment capital and capital equipment, warranty agreements, and schedule and performance issues. A fixed cost contract offers the lowest risk to the customer and generally a low technology risk. A cost plus contract offers the highest financial and product technology risk to the customer. Typically, in shorter term outsourcing that involves a single project, the supplier will not need access to capital and capital equipment, but you should look at several areas to ascertain need. Warranty agreements on software you receive from the supplier can help you avoid costs if serious bugs are found later. Payments and incentives to the supplier should be based on its success at meeting schedule milestones and on other technical performance criteria.

Global companies are increasingly outsourcing software development to other parts within their company. Although some factors (such as the need to state expectations, an examination of schedule and performance options, and investment reviews) still apply, outsourcing within a company requires considering additional factors such as ownership, staffing, and commitment motivators.

4

Dividing the Effort

At some point when using outside software development resources, your company (sometimes together with others) must decide what pieces or activities of the software development should be outsourced. These decisions will come from considering a range of factors—both technical and nontechnical. Depending on the project, the division of effort can be driven by any one or a combination of business relationships, software development phases, architectural considerations, relative knowledge and experience, leadership skills, staffing concerns, tools, and capital investment. Table 4.1 summarizes the characteristics and pros and cons of each basis. I address these in more detail as I describe them.

You may find yourself being motivated by a single factor in certain conditions. For example, staffing may be your only driver when the schedule is extremely tight. In most cases, however, you will be driven by some combination, such as knowledge and experience, architectural concerns, and staffing.

Business Relationships

In strategic partnerships and joint ventures, as well as interdivision efforts within a company, the parties are hoping to gain some benefit, economic or otherwise. How to conduct the effort in a way that will maximize benefit is of great interest and hence many decisions are made before the project starts. Typically, someone has documented how the effort should be divided before the project begins.

Basis for Division of Effort	Pros	Cons	Comments
Business Relations –Percentage of effort/budget –Motivated by technical expertise	–Tied to investment and potential returns –Higher chance of success if technical expertise is leveraged	–May not align with company expertise, potentially risky –May not meet financial objectives	Viewed as investment risk versus rewards versus opportunity costs
Development Phases	Leverage development strengths if companies are aligned with the method. Usually results in higher quality	More communication, may delay project schedule	Usually practiced with smaller companies and on government/ large contracts
Architectural Considerations	Done often; many companies are experienced in this method	Difficult to manage if many functions/objects are outsourced	Used much in industry, functionally dependent
Knowledge and Experience	Lower technical risks, higher efficiency	If not implemented by major subsystems, more difficult to manage	Usually tied to specific areas of responsibility

Basis for Division of Effort	Pros	Cons	Comments
Leadership	Good leaders make a significant difference	Leadership may not line up with organization's technical capability	Considered more when major investments are made in the project
Staffing	Make more progress earlier on the project	If staff knowledge and experience not aligned with functions to be implemented, learning curve will be longer	On projects with tight schedules, usually done by default
Tools and Capital Resources	Tools and resources not a limiting factor during software development	Sometimes the company with the tools and resources is not the one that knows how to best use them	Related to business relationships and tied to investments

Table 4.1: Different methods of dividing the software effort.

When business relationships are the driving factor, effort is allocated in one of two ways:

- *As a percentage of business volume or budget.* The parties agree on the amount of the software effort or budget each will receive, as opposed to identifying who will work on which subsystems. The amount received depends on the amount each is willing to invest. Usually it also depends on the management structure in place, such as the board of directors. It can also depend on political factors, especially during negotiations. In most cases, there is a one-to-one correspondence of percentage invested to percentage of project received. An exception is when one company has a scarce technology (such as one protected by patents) and can thus negotiate a larger percentage of the project than its investment percentage.

In all cases, the immediate motivating factor is how total monies will be divided. What part of the system each will oversee is decided later. For example, in an $18 million communications project between Americo Software Systems and Eurobyte Corp. (fictitious companies), Americo is willing to undertake about 66 percent of the project cost; Eurobyte only 34 percent. Thus, the companies could agree that, since Americo is shouldering most of the financial risk, it will get $12 million and Eurobyte will receive the remaining $6 million.

- *Motivated by area of expertise.* The parties look at areas of technical expertise in deciding financial arrangements. The one that contributes the most technical expertise will receive the greater share of the profits. Assume the same two companies in the previous example have decided to use expertise as a basis for dividing the effort. The companies agree that Americo will develop the user interface and database because it already has a popular user interface that could be partially reused for this project, while Eurobyte will develop the communications and network layer software because it has a strong technical background in these areas. The companies could thus decide that the financial allocation will be Americo, $10 million, and Eurobyte, $8 million.

Even though Americo is investing more capital, Americo and Eurobyte decide on the second option because Eurobyte's technical expertise is vital to the project. Had Eurobyte been less valuable technically, the first option would have been more suitable. In most cases, the division of effort is related to the functionality of the software each company brings with their expertise, but in some cases, the division of expertise can be separated from the project cost. A company may contribute its expertise just to get market exposure, for example, and thus be willing to take less of the profit.

The advantage of work divided purely as a percentage of business volume or budget is that the anticipated effort reflects financial objectives. There is seldom an overcommitment to resources, for example. The advantage of considering technical expertise in a business-relationship-based allocation is that the technical risk during development is lower. Generally, it is best to use the first option when all parties have significant depth in resources and the second option when there is a short time-to-market or when one party has an overwhelming superiority in a technology.

Development Phases

Another approach is to divide effort by development life-cycle phase. In many large projects, the participating companies have certain specialties—software system design, integration and test, customer support, and so on—which can serve as the basis for allocation across the life cycle. Figure 4.1 gives a possible allocation, in which four companies participate.

Returning to the two fictitious companies, Eurobyte has designed high-speed data communications systems for commercial applications but now wants to enter the government market. Americo is a strong software validation company with current government contracts. The companies decide that Eurobyte will do requirements and design, Americo will do the software testing and customer support, and both companies will do the implementation. This approach is most cost-effective in large software development efforts, but medium and even some smaller efforts are beginning to use this approach because they recognize the value of making products that meet all the customer expectations. In some cases, the best way to achieve that level of quality is to use companies that specialize in a particular life-cycle phase, such as testing.

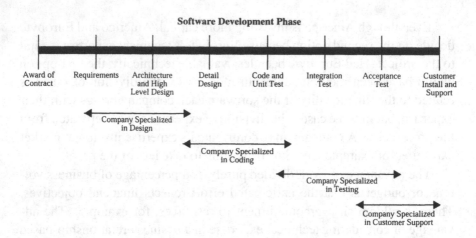

Figure 4.1: Outsourcing different phases of software development.

The advantage of this approach is that companies specializing in a particular phase, such as validation, tend to be more productive. The disadvantage is that you have to maintain deliverables from that phase, such as requirements and design documents, after the project is over. If you must maintain documents you didn't produce and have no access to their author, you may misinterpret their content.

Architectural Considerations

This is probably the most often used basis for dividing effort in outsourced projects. Figure 4.2 illustrates how it applies the divide-and-conquer principle. In this example, the company that is responsible for delivering the product divides the system into the subsystems that must be developed. The companies jointly decide to outsource the scheduler and communications software subsystems and their functionality to companies with more knowledge and experience.

This approach has been used for decades. The advantage is that you can cleanly segregate the outsourcing effort because each subsystem performs unique functions and either is isolated or has well-defined interfaces to the rest of the system. It is also easier to successfully manage discrete efforts than highly coupled ones.

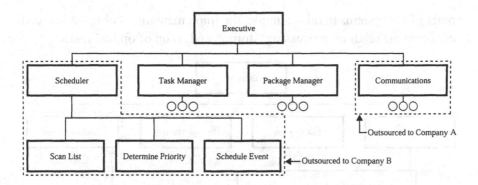

Figure 4.2: Dividing effort along architecture considerations.

The disadvantage is that you will require considerable effort to manage interface specifications between subsystems.

Knowledge and Experience

Using knowledge and experience in a technology as a basis for dividing work is also popular. This approach is not quite the same as technical expertise driven by business relationships because, in most cases, it is used when companies need services that are difficult to obtain; whereas the technical expertise as part of a business relationship focuses mainly on financial arrangements. The more knowledge and experience a company has, typically the more efficient they are and the higher the product quality. Dividing effort along the lines of the supplier's knowledge and experience also represents a lower technical cost and schedule risk to outsourcing and management.

The company responsible for delivering the product again draws up an architectural diagram. This time, however, as Figure 4.3 shows, effort can be divided as both a horizontal and vertical slice of the architecture, as opposed to just a vertical slice when architecture is the only basis (see Figure 4.2). As in the architectural division, the vertical slice represents the functionality that closely matches a supplier's knowledge and experience. The horizontal approach is more related to knowledge and experience in implementation. These types of tasks may be required to produce several parts of the system. In this example, the implementation being outsourced concerns the reading, processing, storing, and so on of optical disks.

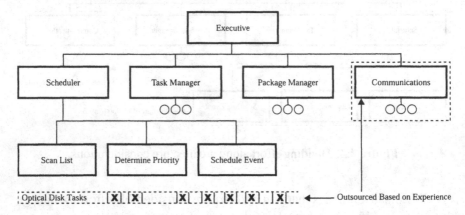

Figure 4.3: Dividing effort based on knowledge and experience.

Both vertical and horizontal slicing according to knowledge and experience are suitable for structured design approaches based on system functions. More recent design approaches, such as object orientation, are less likely to find vertical slices that represent a supplier's knowledge and experience. Outsourcing based on knowledge and experience is also more difficult to implement and manage with OO.

Leadership

Although not overtly recognized, some decisions to divide software effort for outsourcing are based on leadership. These are companies with proven people skills and technical competence.

Outsourcing software to a company with a proven leadership record may not be enough to offset certain risks. I recommend asking three questions:

- *Does the company understand the problem and have a vision for its solution?* One way to measure this is to look at the company's ability to grasp secondary issues. For example, if the outsourcing involves creating an embedded software for industrial use, does the company understand the effects of timing and interrupt handling for diagnostic routines? The company must also be able to validate its assumptions. If the company understands the problem and has a vision of its solution, it may be just as valuable as a company with a higher degree of technical knowledge and experience but average leadership. As the customer, your schedule risks will be mitigated because the company will not be going down the wrong technical path.

- *Does the company have the resources to perform the work?* This may seem obvious, but I've seen numerous organizations assume the supplier can handle the outsourcing, only to find midway through the project that it needs more staff, tools, or facilities or the schedule will suffer. In a large development effort, track records on smaller tasks may not be a good indicator. Be sure that the company has had some experience handling the demands of a larger project.

- *Is the company committed to following through on the work?* Track records of any kind are valuable here. However, even if the company has demonstrated success managing multiple projects, commitment to your outsourced software project may be low if it does not represent a significant portion of the supplier's business. You can determine a supplier's commitment level by asking what percentage of its sales are based on your business. You can also ask how many full-time staff it plans to commit to the project.

The advantage of dividing effort in this manner is that you reduce your risk that the outsourcing will fail. The entire decision to outsource is based on the ability of the organization, or leaders in that organization, to get the job completed despite known and unknown impediments [1]. The disadvantage is that even with good leadership, a project may fail if there is a lack of resources or commitment from higher management.

Staffing

When the schedule is tight, staffing may be the primary basis for dividing the effort. It may also be a consideration if the companies want to use their combined staffing more efficiently. In Figure 4.4, for example, Company A brings five qualified project members; Company B only three. Company A draws up an architectural diagram and the companies decide to put Company A's staff on the largest subsystems.

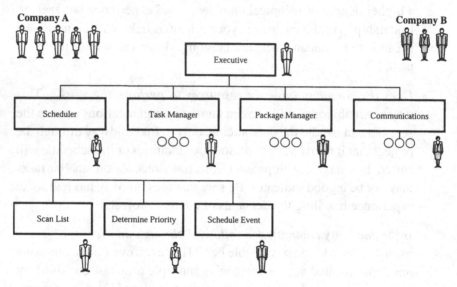

Figure 4.4: Allocating staff to architecture.

The advantage of this method is that it reduces schedule risks because the largest tasks are assigned to the company with the most resources. The disadvantage is that if staff knowledge and experience are not aligned with functions to implement, the learning curve will be longer.

Tools and Capital Resources

Similar to dividing effort according to staffing, effort can be divided according to software tools and capital development availability, such as facilities, investment capital, and computers. If staffing is equal, the company with more and better tools and capital resources, or the potential to acquire them, is usually given the larger share of the software effort.

Tools and capital provide a leverage against risk because they can increase productivity, quality, and the ability to handle unexpected problems.

Companies that have better tools and capital resources are usually more productive and able to keep closer to schedule and budget. I say "usually" because you can always encounter a company with a vast array of tools and only a vague idea of how to use them productively. To determine a company's tool proficiency, ask how long they've used the tools, look at their past projects, and ask them to frankly assess the strengths and weaknesses of the tools.

Key Thoughts

Companies can divide effort in many ways, depending on individual circumstances. If business relationships are the basis, there is the further option of dividing the project purely as a percentage of effort or budget or with technical expertise in mind. Companies that use this basis are typically more focused on financial concerns.

Effort can also be divided by development phase. In this approach, the companies doing the outsourcing specialize in particular tasks such as requirements generation or validation, which often means they are more productive. The disadvantage is that you have to maintain deliverables from that phase, such as requirements and design documents, which you may not fully understand.

Dividing effort by architectural considerations is the most popular approach. Because a company is responsible for an entire subsystem, there is a clean division of responsibility. Each subsystem performs unique functions and either is isolated or has well-defined interfaces to the rest of the system. The disadvantage is the difficulty in managing the interface specifications between subsystems.

Leadership is also a basis for dividing effort but a company's leadership may not be enough to offset other weaknesses. The company should understand the problem and have a vision for its solution, have the resources to perform the work, and be committed to following through with their part of the project. The advantage of this approach is that you reduce the risk of failure; the disadvantage is that you may be relying too heavily on one attribute of the company.

When a project is on a tight deadline, staffing may be the only viable basis for dividing effort. It can also be used to start a project more quickly if one company has many more staff than another.

Finally, companies can divide effort according to which has the most tool expertise and most capital investment. If staffing is equal, the company with more and better tools and capital resources, or the potential to acquire them, is usually given the larger share of the software effort. However, just having tools does not guarantee that they are being used correctly. The company should have used the tools on past projects and be familiar with their strengths and weaknesses.

Bibliography

[1] R. Grenier and G. Metes, *Going Virtual*, Prentice Hall, Upper Saddle River, NJ, 1995.

5

Responsibility and Accountability

An important task—and one easily overlooked—is determining responsibilities and accountabilities among companies. *Responsibility* is the act of performing a task and the resulting actions, such as designing a piece of software to meet a schedule milestone. *Accountability* is acknowledging ownership of the activity regardless of who performed the tasks, such as delivering a quality piece of outsourced software.

Responsibility and accountability have many facets—all of which are far-reaching. It's no surprise that this is one of the longer chapters in the book. If done properly, responsibility and accountability activities will help you avoid many of the major problems associated with global software development. Defining roles, specifying what to do when there are conflicts, outlining communication paths, and setting expectations help overcome differences in culture, business style, methodologies, and practices people mistakenly assume everyone does the same way. The goal is to set a strong foundation of communications and structure. The project team will then be free to focus on solving technical problems and making a product that will satisfy its end users.

Determining and Documenting Expectations

The first step in arriving at a common set of expectations is to identify differences between team members and partners. When responsibility and accountability issues are global, this involves looking at how different cultures react to social situations, work pressure, and other important issues. You should do this well before you begin the project so that everyone is aware of these differences. The milestone chart in Appendix B of this book shows when this activity should begin.

Cultural Differences

When interfacing and managing people from other than North American cultures, remember that

- *Some cultures do not promote individual responsibility and account-ability.* The emphasis may be on consensus, which tends to delay decision-making, relative to Western business practices. You'll need to recognize this practice and plan your expectations accordingly.

- *Some cultures accept most suggestions without much discussion.* Even though they disagree, they will not be open about it because open conflict is not encouraged. In this case, the best strategy is to touch base with one or two individuals in a social setting to understand their concerns.

- *If things appear to be too good to be true, they probably are.* In some cultures, it is acceptable not to admit problems or mistakes unless you have no choice. In this case, dig for additional information by seeking evidence that validates the outside assertions.

Above all, do not assume that the motivations, actions, and reasoning of those from other countries match yours. Several excellent texts describe how to do business in different countries [1, 2, 3, 4, 5]. I recommend reading any of them to familiarize yourself with the habits of other cultures. Failing to recognize these differences can have some serious consequences. For example, in a joint software partnership with a US team and one in central Europe, each month after the project started, the status meetings showed that everything was on schedule—even though requirements were changing. No one questioned the European reports. However, when joint design reviews began, the technical information the European partner sent indicated it was far behind what it had reported. The US team had failed to account for the European culture's acceptable practice of minimizing problems.

Issues to Document

It's not enough to merely set expectations. You must be sure that everyone on the project has working documents, such as a statement of work, a list of terms and conditions, requirements specifications, and schedules. Assumptions always create problems. Even talking about expectations—while important—can lead to misinterpretations. A written document is not foolproof, but you get closer to developing software with fewer problems, such as missed tasks or redundant effort.

Written expectations should spell out common project issues and their possible effect on software developers. The rest of the chapter deals with the issues that should be made clear in any set of written expectations—the structure of the virtual organization; schedule and cost; tools and methods; software configuration management; quality control measures; and mechanisms for resolving both technical and business conflicts. This list is based on my experience and is by no means exhaustive.

Virtual Organization Structure

As I mentioned in Chapter 2, you must consider many aspects when setting up a virtual organization. One is the project's organization, which changes as the project evolves. Like the project itself, the structure spans several software development partners but is managed as if it involves only one organization.

Critical in managing a virtual structure is understanding the roles and responsibilities of the project members. Documenting the virtual organization structure, either on paper or electronically, gives management, each project team member, and other project stakeholders a sense of organization and an understanding of individual roles and responsibilities. An electronic version can provide views on multiple levels—for example, the big picture in one view and detailed responsibilities in the other. Users can click on a box to view a short description of the member in charge of that particular part of the organization. Figure 5.1 gives a sample of how different views can be called up. Because of space concerns, only one box shows the complete details, which include title, contact information, and a brief summary of responsibilities.

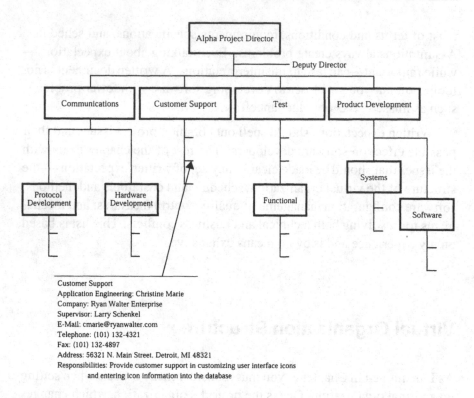

Customer Support
Application Engineering: Christine Marie
Company: Ryan Walter Enterprise
Supervisor: Larry Schenkel
E-Mail: cmarie@ryanwalter.com
Telephone: (101) 132-4321
Fax: (101) 132-4897
Address: 56321 N. Main Street, Detroit, MI 48321
Responsibilities: Provide customer support in customizing user interface icons
                and entering icon information into the database

Figure 5.1: An example of a virtual structure with built-in responsibility descriptions.

Schedule, Cost, and Quality

Responsibility and accountability for schedule, cost, and quality ultimately belong to all project partners. Without a mutual commitment, the project is not likely to succeed. On the other hand, only one partner should be ultimately responsible for monitoring and reporting the status of the project schedule, cost, and quality.

Why shouldn't each partner separately report its own status and be treated as a separate cost structure? This approach, which is all too common, doesn't work any better than having one group for quality, one for cost, and one for schedule. Self-interest can come into play in both cases. A partner may make its responsibilities look better than they actually are or make others look worse. Having one partner monitor and report status is one way to avoid this.

Another reason not to separate the responsibility and accountability of schedule, cost, and quality is that they are interrelated, as Figure 5.2 shows.

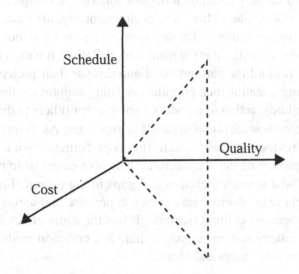

Figure 5.2: The interrelationship between schedule, cost, and quality aspects of a software project.

You cannot slip schedule without affecting cost, and in many cases quality, if you skip or reduce testing to make up the lost time. Investing in additional tools and personnel will affect schedule by increasing the training time. Later, it will (hopefully) increase both productivity and quality, since fewer problems will be introduced and some will be avoided altogether. Problems in testing may occur because of a quality slippage in earlier stages. This will affect schedule because the errors are more serious at this stage and require more time to fix. Cost is also higher for the same reason.

Normally, the responsibility and accountability for these aspects of a software project fall on the project manager. In some cases, the project manager can appoint someone to oversee responsibility and report to him. I talk more about the project manager's specific responsibilities in Chapter 7.

Tools and Methods

The responsibility and accountability for procuring tools usually reside with each partner as part of the investment to perform the work. The responsibility to identify common tools and software development methods, however, should reside within one development organization. That does not mean having someone in that organization define what tools and methods should be used without input from others. Rather, it means having representatives from all the partners meet and discuss their preferences. The responsible organization then provides on-going support for the agreed-on tools and methods, acting as a pool of expertise for others to draw on.

Having common tools and methods is important. As the project begins to integrate, reviews are held, and testing is performed, so it is much easier to get a picture of the architecture. It is also easier to implement the software without structural clashes and gaps in the design. Finally, commonality in these areas provides a common practice that unites developers across language and cultural barriers. It has the same effect as choosing a common implementation language: there is a common medium through which to express thoughts and ideas.

Software Configuration Management

Assigning responsibility and accountability is, in part, a way to help control the software project as it unfolds. As is true in a nonvirtual project, the use of common *software configuration management* practices on a virtual project will help ensure control over both documentation and software. SCM has the same philosophy as traditional configuration management, but its implementation involves tools and methods unique to controlling software.

SCM basically ensures that changes to the software are managed. In a nonvirtual development environment, it is considered good practice to apply established SCM tools and techniques [6]. However, they are just beginning to be used in virtual software development.

One reason is that, while virtual environments have many of the same problems common in nonvirtual environments, they also give rise to unique challenges:

- *How to manage different changes at different sites as one product.* It can be difficult to control the changes within each location and coordinate each location's change process with total product development across multiple sites. The changes at each site must be coordinated according to the schedule for that site, but they must also be viewed in the context of their effect on the total project schedule.

- *How to apply standards consistently.* Maintaining the consistency of standards application—such as enforcing when to release software, what documentation format to use, or how to approve changes—is more difficult in a virtual organization. Different sites tend to interpret the standards according to their culture and local interests. Written expectations should make it clear how standards should be applied so that everyone is working from the same interpretation. Wrong assumptions can lead to a misapplication of the standard, which can show up as problems during integration and test. This in turn can delay releasing the product, which hurts all parties. The consistent application of standards assures the customer that the software has gone through an acceptable process, no matter where it was developed.

- *How to incorporate changes in a timely manner.* Challenges here include how to coordinate changes into different software builds, make different versions work together, and ensure that everything follows the process in an acceptable timeframe. With changes going through a local software configuration control board, and then through additional reviews at the location where the software is integrated, this is much more difficult than in a nonvirtual organization, where changes are managed in one location.

All these issues must be addressed through a *virtual software configuration management board* that reports to a centralized *software configuration control manager*. In this structure, a single body accepts responsibility and accountability for the process and common CM tools. There is then accountability and revision control over several aspects, including

- *Important documentation.* Control over requirements specifications, designs, test plans, and so on is even more important in a virtual project because of the many changes within and among different locations—all of which must be managed.

- *Source code and software tools delivered to the end user.* This is important because you may need to trace errors to the outsourced software to satisfy contract arrangements (see Chapter 2).

- *Changes approved and made to documentation and software.* This is important because uncontrolled or disapproved changes will cause errors, which will delay project completion and needlessly tie up resources.

Having one person be responsible and accountable for managing and controlling these activities is most important during the integration phase because documentation and software change will occur at multiple locations. A strong SCM process will also help overcome differences in management styles and cultural interpretations by enforcing a common discipline and set of expectations for documentation and change handling. An SCM plan that documents the expectations of all team members is an extremely useful tool.

I describe both the SCM board and SCM plan in more detail in Chapter 7.

Quality Control

Quality must be built into the software. Most mature software development organizations have processes and structures in place to promote quality. These organizations share certain attitudes and conceptions about what it takes to produce quality software, including a recognition that

- *Software quality is influenced by the development process.* The development process can increase repeatability and reduce variability. Repeatability is increased because a process tends to repeat tasks until they yield a satisfactory result. This allows good practices to be transferred from developers' thoughts into written standards and guidelines that others can benefit from. Variability is reduced because by following standards and guidelines, developers avoid repeating mistakes or making false assumptions, thus producing better estimates of schedule and effort. They are also able to select a measurement system that more accurately indicates the quality level.

- *Software quality is influenced by how the software is designed.* A good software process alone will not guarantee high-quality software. The design strategy influences expendability, maintainability, testing, reliability, and error recovery. Recognizing that software will change and must recover from error conditions, the software design should incorporate a structure to allow flexibility and a robustness to gracefully continue processing during expected and unexpected error conditions.

- *Software quality must be measured.* A measurement system that identifies what constitutes quality shows that a company is focused on understanding its quality problems. Quality indicators can be the number of software problems customers report, internal software problem reports, or different categories of error types. Another aspect of quality measurement is the commitment to act on the measurement system. Corrective actions and improvement activities should be based on the results of using the system.

- *Software quality is tightly linked to customer satisfaction.* When a company identifies a link between customer satisfaction and software quality, quality initiatives are noticeably visible. There is a willingness to invest in software process development, measurement, self and outside audits, and continued software improvement.

When considering software quality in a global market, you must be aware of various software quality standards that products must meet. Appendix C lists some major international software quality standards used in industry and government. A more complete list of software development and quality standards is available in *Guide to Software Engineering Standards and Specifications* [7].

Metrics

Metrics measure the software product or process. In a virtual project, as in most large projects, the ability to quantifiably judge the project's status lets

you more accurately assess the team's progress and the software's quality.
Elsewhere I give an overview of using metrics in a large project [8].

Process metrics measure the effectiveness of the development process.
Metrics in this category include risk management metrics, metrics related
to quality such as the number of defects found at each phase of the development process, adherence to the development process, and the effort and
time spent developing the software.

Product metrics measure software attributes, such as complexity, reliability, and quality. Some product metrics, such as complexity metrics,
are based on the source code. They can measure the number of noncom-
mented source code statements, function points, the number of opcodes or
operands, or the number of branches. Figure 5.3 shows a code complexity
metric that measures the number of branches.

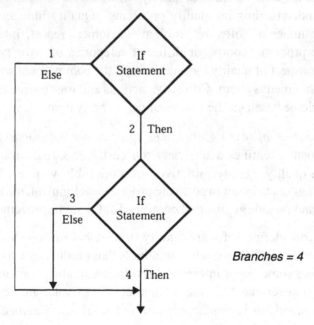

Figure 5.3: Example of code complexity using branches.

With metrics, you can see if more investigation is needed into various
aspects of development and the product. For example, if metrics collected
in later development phases show a high frequency of errors, the product

may require more extensive testing before it is delivered. If very few errors are found early in testing, you may need to augment the existing test methods or use other methods.

Problem Reports

Problem reports are a way to formally capture problems, review them, track them, and close them. Problem reports, detailed descriptions of the problems found, increase quality control because they identify issues that need attention, either in the software itself or in its application or documentation. Figure 5.4 shows a sample software problem report.

The key fields in the problem report are

- *Project name or number.* Identifies the software project or product that has the problem.

- *Report number.* Used to reference and log the report.

- *Date.* Day the problem was identified.

- *Originator.* Person who identified the problem.

- *Software name.* Identifies the software module, document, or process that has the problem (if known).

- *Baseline version:* Identifies the software's configuration version.

- *Method of identification.* Identifies the development phase during which the problem was identified; used for metric reporting.

- *Severity of problem:* Classifies the problem to help determine its priority; also used in metric reporting.

- *System impact.* Identifies the part of the system the problem affects (if known).

- *Action.* Identifies if the problem report is disapproved, or if approved, who it is assigned to for correction.

- *Description.* Textual description of the problem or symptom.

DATE:	**Software Problem Report**	PROJECT NAME OR NUMBER:	REPORT NUMBER:
ORIGINATOR:		SOFTWARE NAME:	BASELINE VERSION:

METHOD OF IDENTIFICATION: (Check one of the following)
- ☐ Requirements Review ☐ Design Review ☐ Code Review
- ☐ Integration Test ☐ Acceptance Test ☐ Customer
- ☐ Other (please define)

SEVERITY OF PROBLEM: (Check one of the following)
- ☐ Critical Function ☐ Affects or Degrades Critical Function
- ☐ Non-critical Function ☐ Critical Function with Work-Around
- ☐ Other (please define)

SYSTEM IMPACT: (Check all that apply)
- ☐ Algorithm ☐ Diagnostics ☐ Operating System ☐ Communications ☐ Other (please describe below)

ACTION: (Check appropriate boxes)   ☐ Disapproved   ☐ Approved by Lead Software Engineer and Assigned to:

DESCRIPTION:

ANALYSIS:

RESOLUTION:

VERIFICATION SECTION:

IMPLEMENTED BY:	DATE:	RELEASE VERSION:
VERIFIED BY:	DATE:	VERIFICATION REF.:
INSTALLED IN VERSION:	DATE:	

CHANGE ACCEPTANCE:

ORIGINATOR:	DATE:
MANAGER:	DATE:
OTHER:	DATE:

Figure 5.4: Sample software problem report.

- *Analysis.* Textual description of how to approach fixing the problem.

- *Resolution.* Textual description of the results of fixing the problem and the subsequent test.

- *Verification section.* Identifies who fixed the problem, who tested the solution, what version of software it was installed in ("installed in version" in the figure), and what verification report was involved.

- *Change acceptance.* Contains the signature of the person who found the problem, the next level supervisor, and others, such as the quality manager, or SCM representative.

When the software is released, problem reports are invaluable for maintaining and debugging it. You should maintain a central library of problem report logs and problem reports as the project nears completion. A log typically contains an entry for each problem report, including the problem name, number, and date.

Conflict Resolution

Responsibility and accountability mean that there must be some mechanism for handling conflict resolution and a person who ultimately decides that resolution. There are two major categories of conflicts: technical and business.

Technical Conflicts

Conflicts in design approaches and design implementation are inevitable when development spans several organizations. Most of these problems usually work themselves out. However, in some cases disagreements make their way up the chain of command, so there must be a central *design authority* to resolve them.

The design authority is the last place to appeal a technical decision. The organization must entrust this authority to an individual who will call the final shots in a timely and an unbiased manner. The individual must balance the need for all members to be heard with the need to keep technical progress on schedule.

For larger projects, several deputy design authorities may also be appointed, each with a limited domain over a particular set of technical functions or disciplines. There could be a design authority for user interfaces, one for protocol development, and one for signal processing, for example. These authorities would indirectly report to the overall design authority. Deputy design authorities resemble a court system, with the overall design authority being the highest court.

Business Conflicts

Many nontechnical conflicts will also arise in a global or virtual environment. These include decisions about payment or investment, schedule, meeting places or arrangements (travel), authority, partitioning of responsibilities, and new or not previously identified tasks. This list is by no means exhaustive. There may be many more, depending on the type of business arrangement.

No matter what the business arrangements, however, a single person should be accountable and responsible to ensure these types of conflicts are resolved and do not hold up the project's progress. The most qualified person is the project manager because in most organizations the project manager is the one held accountable for commercial and budgetary issues.

Key Thoughts

Responsibility and accountability, if done properly, will avoid many major problems associated with global software development. *Responsibility* is the act of performing a task and the resulting actions, such as designing a piece of software to a schedule milestone. *Accountability* is accepting ownership of the activity regardless of who performed the tasks, such as delivering a quality piece of outsourced software.

Defining expectations is a first step in handling responsibility and accountability. Remember that different cultures have different work philosophies, social etiquettes, and expectations. Discuss these before the project begins and document them on paper or electronically so that everyone can access them. Issues that should be spelled out in any set of written expectations include the structure of the virtual organization; schedule, cost, and quality; tools and methods; software configuration management; development process; and mechanisms for resolving both technical and business conflicts.

Documenting the virtual organization structure, either on paper or electronically, gives everyone a unified sense of individual roles and responsibilities. In issues of schedule, cost, and quality, keeping responsibility and accountability within a single company (or in some cases, individual) prevents self-interested parties from distorting their responsibilities and putting others in a bad light. It also helps preserve the interrelationship of the three concerns.

Having one organization take responsibility for supporting the tools and agreed-on software development methods helps provide a foundation of common practices as well as a base of expertise for the entire project team.

Centralized responsibility and accountability for the software configuration management process and tools helps provide accountability and revision control over deliverables and change handling.

Quality control is an important aspect of accountability. It should recognize that quality is influenced by the development process, the design choices, the quality indicators chosen, and customer satisfaction. As part of good quality management, establish metrics. *Process* metrics measure the effectiveness of the development process. *Product* metrics measure software attributes, such as complexity, reliability, and quality. Problem reports are also important tools for identifying issues that need attention, either in the software itself or in its application or documentation.

Finally, conflicts in a global development are inevitable. For technical conflicts, have a central design authority as the last mechanism for appeal. For business conflicts, such as payment, new tasks, and authority issues, use the project manager.

Bibliography

[1] S.P. Dunung, *Doing Business in Asia: The Complete Guide*, The Free Press, New York, 1994.

[2] L.W. Tuller, *Doing Business in Latin America & the Caribbean: Including Mexico, the U.S. Virgin Islands & Puerto Rico, Central America, South America*, AMACOM, New York, 1993.

[3] M. Johnson and R.T. Moran, *Cultural Guide to Doing Business in Europe*, Butterworth-Heinemann, Oxford, UK, 1992.

[4] P. Kenna and S. Lacy, *Business Japan: A Practical Guide to Understanding Japanese Business Culture*, NTC Publishing Group, Sumas, Wash., 1994.

[5] K.B. Bucknall, *Cultural Guide to Doing Business in China*, Butterworth-Heinemann, Oxford, UK, 1994.

[6] R. Berlack, *Software Configuration Management*, Wiley & Sons, New York, 1991.

[7] S. Magee and L. Tripp, *Guide to Software Engineering Standards and Specifications*, Artech House, Norwood, Mass., 1997.

[8] D. Karolak, "Identifying Software Quality Metrics for a Large Software Development," *Proc. IEEE GlobeCom'85*, IEEE Press, New York, 1985, pp. 61–64.

6

Effective Communication

When managing software-development projects at diverse locations, communications methods and tools offer one of the most powerful and effective ways to gather and disseminate information and control the project. In effective communication, people not only send and receive verbal or text messages, but nonverbal indicators make it easier for the receiver to interpret the message's intent and for the sender to ascertain that the message was received and understood.

To determine if a communication method is effective, you need to look at two dimensions: timeliness and content. *Timeliness* is how quickly the communication is received. *Content* is the amount of verbal or written communication, and what can be read into it, such as through facial expressions (in a face-to-face meeting), tone of voice, or voice inflections. Figure 6.1 lists the most popular communication methods for conducting global software development and shows their positions along the timeliness and content axes.

Communication methods that rate high on the content axis, such as face to face, have both verbal and nonverbal content. Communication methods that rate high on the timeliness axis, such as telephone conferences, offer either real-time or very near real-time interaction (as measured by when the receiver receives the sender's message).

Figure 6.2 shows how each method differs in timeliness and content using a simple communication model that involves a sender, receiver, and single message (depicted by an arrow). As the figure shows, the communication characteristics change, depending on the type of communication. The shorter the arrow between sender and receiver, the closer they are to real-time communication. The larger the area within the arrow, the greater the communication content. The darker the area, the clearer the communication.

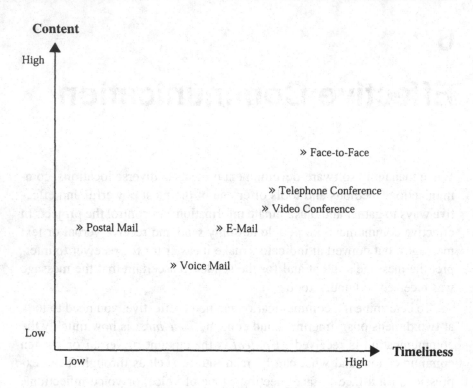

Figure 6.1: Effectiveness of communications methods.

I will refer to parts of this figure as I describe each communication type, from most to least effective. Jessica Lipnack and Jeffrey Stamps give additional views of communication methods and their relationship to virtual teams [1].

Face-to-Face

There is no substitute for face-to-face meetings. As Figure 6.2a shows, the message is both in real time and has a large amount of content. In this communication type, the receiver most effectively understands both the message and its intent. During a conversation, messages are formed, communicated, interpreted, responded to, and clarified. With this rich interaction, communicators can grasp the message with little misunderstanding.

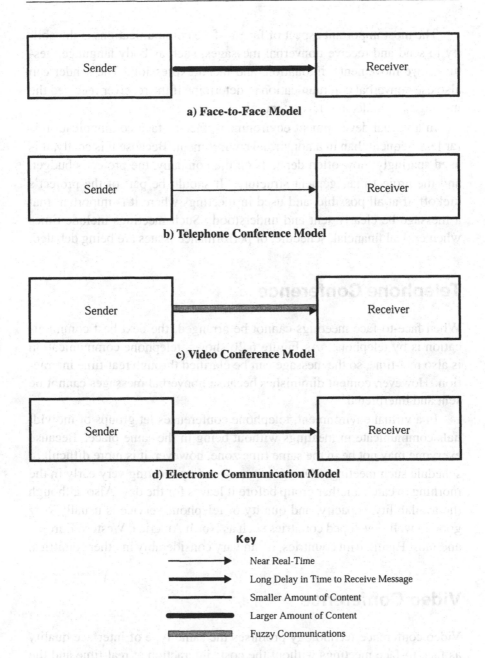

Figure 6.2: Communication models and their effectiveness.

The most important aspect of face-to-face communications is the ability to send and receive nonverbal messages, such as body language, gestures, eye movements, intonation, and facial expression. The sender can also use nonverbal communication to determine if the receiver received the message and understood its intent.

In a virtual development environment, face-to-face communication is far less frequent than in a nonvirtual environment. Because it is costly, it is used sparingly; how often depends on the company, the project's budget, and the project management structure. It should be part of the project's kickoff, if at all possible, and used in meetings where it is important that a message be clearly sent and understood. Such meetings include times when critical financial, schedule, or performance issues are being debated.

Telephone Conference

When face-to-face meetings cannot be arranged, the next best communication is by telephone. As Figure 6.2b shows, telephone communication is also real-time, so the message can be clarified through real-time interaction. However, content diminishes because nonverbal messages cannot be sent and interpreted.

In a virtual environment, telephone conferences let groups of individuals communicate in meetings without being in the same place. Because everyone may not be in the same time zone, however, it is more difficult to schedule such meetings. One group may end up meeting very early in the morning to catch another group before it leaves for the day. Also, although the availability, capacity, and quality of telephone service is usually very good in well-developed countries such as North America, Western Europe, and most Pacific Rim countries, it can vary considerably in other countries.

Video Conference

Video conference technology promises the same type of interface quality as face-to-face meetings without the cost: interaction at real-time and the sending and receiving of nonverbal messages.

As Figure 6.2c shows, the only difference between video conferencing and face-to-face communications is the quality of the communication. The inherent transmission delays between speech and video make video conference communications that involve movement (such as a stand-up presentation) less effective than a face-to-face meeting. Likewise, transmission delays mean that communication becomes more script-like, in that each person talks and then waits for a response; there is no overlapping conversation. As transmission delays continue to diminish, this artificial environment will hopefully improve.

The availability of this technology is also an issue, especially outside the US. It is still expensive to purchase transmission bandwidth and the proper equipment. As the information superhighway infrastructure continues to build worldwide, this type of technology should become more widely available via the Internet, and personal computer vendors will intensify efforts to add video conference peripherals to PCs. Until these problems are addressed on a large scale, however, face-to-face and telephone communications will continue to be more effective media for the virtual development team.

Electronic Communication

The most popular means of communicating in a virtual organization is electronically—via the Web, local area network, or electronic bulletin boards. Figure 6.2d shows the model for electronic communication.

The Web and Internet

For a distributed organization, it is most efficient to communicate electronically using an existing communication structure. The Web and Internet offer a maintained structure that costs very little to use, relative to setting up your own wide area network. One way to use the Web is to set up a Web site where team members can get and leave information about the project.

The major disadvantage of this is that anyone can access whatever you place on the Web site—the primary reason electronic communication is not widely used for virtual projects. However, Web security can be improved through the use of encryption.

Electronic mail through the Internet, supplemented with encryption, is a more secure option. E-mail provides a means of fast written communications, and unauthorized users cannot easily compromise the privacy of the message. It is also a convenient way to set up mailing lists and directions for correspondence and electronic filing. The down side is that there is no guarantee of near-real-time communication because conditions on the Internet are unpredictable.

Dedicated WANs and LANs

In a virtual team environment, the most efficient and secure way to communicate in a written format is through a dedicated *wide area network* and *local area network*. The communication model of a dedicated WAN and LAN shares many of the characteristics of the model for the Web and Internet (such as global electronic access to team members and information sharing), but there are also distinct differences.

Unlike the Web and Internet, the organization controls much of the communication transmission aspects. Because lines are dedicated, transmission speed and quality (bandwidth and reception) can be more tightly controlled.

WANs and LANs also let you control security. Unlike the Web and Internet, access to your information does not require extremely complex security measures, such as encryption, because the networks cannot be accessed by just anyone. However, some security measures, such as user or system passwords, are still required to ensure that unauthorized users do not compromise the network's integrity.

There is also more control over reliability and access with a dedicated WAN and LAN. Unlike the Web and Internet, which are open to public use and misuse, the organization pays for a dedicated WAN and LAN and its users are not likely to abuse it. It is in the organization's best interests to keep the network service optimum—fast access is practically guaranteed. No one can guarantee consistently optimum service on the Web and Internet.

On the down side, a WAN and LAN cost significantly more to set up and use than simply accessing the Web and Internet. For most companies, the cost of the capital equipment, leased lines, software, and on-going maintenance for a dedicated WAN and LAN is prohibitive.

Likewise, the cost of personnel to maintain and troubleshoot the network may be prohibitive. Significant effort may be involved to keep availability, reliability, and access at a level the network's users find acceptable.

Another disadvantage of dedicated WANs and LANs is that special accounts must be set up and maintained if vendors or others outside the team want to interact with team members. This adds administrative overhead for both the company and the vendor.

Electronic Bulletin Boards

Although not as popular today, electronic bulletin boards are very cost effective, requiring only a PC, a telephone line, and inexpensive bulletin board software.

Their main disadvantage is the type of interaction, which is basically leaving messages to be read later. It is inconvenient to have to log on to check for messages, and only a few people can use the system at any one time because of traffic on the telephone lines.

Other Considerations

Communication in a distributed virtual environment is not confined to the amount and timeliness of the message; it also involves considerations such as cultural aspects and time differences. These other considerations affect how the message is sent, how it is interpreted, and what action will result.

Cultural Differences

As I mentioned in Chapters 2 and 5, it is important to research and interact with cultures represented in your team. In communications, it is then easier to select the most effective communication means and methods.

Verbal responses and body language may be interpreted differently than in Western cultures, for example. Eastern cultures do not deal openly with confrontational issues. When people receive a message they disagree with or don't like, they will give no response or rebuttal. If you are not aware of this cultural communication difference, you may believe the message was well received. In Eastern cultures, the person may go so far as to agree with you but have no intention of following through—a behavior that is perfectly acceptable in those cultures. There are many such differences, and team members should acquaint themselves with them if communication is to be effective [2, 3, 4, 5, 6].

Time Differences

When and how you communicate will also be influenced by time differences. Anyone who has dealt with communications over time-zone differences of three hours or more knows that real-time communication can take place only during a few hours of the workday.

Communication over large time-zone differences can also be affected by the physical and mental states of the participants; those at one location may be just starting their day while others are ending the day and are perhaps exhausted. Sometimes, decisions must be delayed because someone has left early during the day the real-time communication takes place.

In many cases, e-mail, faxes, and bulletin boards are good supplements for correspondence during off hours because they alert the other team members that some action is required before the next telephone or video contact. It is a good idea to agree on a few hours each day that all team members will be available for real-time contact.

On-the-fly adjustments are an important part of communications in a virtual team. You may use e-mail one day, a fax the next, and real-time telephoning the next. Team members need to be made aware of each other's needs and to have communications resources they can configure as needed.

Organizing Communications

The amount of information communicated electronically can easily become overwhelming. Managers can easily have 20 to 40 messages when they log on each morning—and most are forwards or cc's. This is a common problem because the technology makes it so easy to copy and forward information quickly. It is important to have an organized system for responding to messages. One manager I knew structured his workday to respond to all communications, from real-time to non-real-time. He addressed voice mail first, and then in descending order, e-mail, faxes, internal mail, and external mail. His reasoning was that if people really wanted to contact him about important items, this is probably the order they would also use.

Groupware packages can help the team manage the volume of mail by letting the user file, delete, sort, and filter e-mail. In a distributed virtual team environment, an investment in this type of software is well worth it. Mellanie Hills [7] and Joanne Woodcock [8] give good overviews of groupware software concepts and their implementation.

Security

Security is important to keep outside people from gaining access to your communications and to keep internal people from gaining access to sensitive information.

Standard groupware packages allow a good measure of security for LANs. I recommend considering additional security measures, such as encryption, for electronic and video communication outside the physical facility (for WANs). With the increase of industrial espionage, the cost of establishing such a mechanism should be weighed against the benefit of preventing data vandalism or interception. There are many excellent texts on network security [9, 10].

Key Thoughts

Communications methods and tools offer one of the most powerful and effective ways to gather and disseminate information and control the project. Communication can be characterized by *timeliness*—how quickly the communication is received—and *content*—the amount of verbal or written communication, and what can be read into it through nonverbal communication such as facial expressions.

Communication methods provide varying degrees of the two characteristics. *Face-to-face meetings* provide both real-time interaction and high content. *Telephone conferences* are the next most effective method, but nonverbal communication is eliminated, so content suffers. *Video conferences* are promising, but transmission delays make real-time interaction difficult. Also, the required equipment is too costly for many organizations. Web access is an inexpensive option, but security is a problem because anyone can access a Web site. Encrypted *e-mail* through the Internet is more secure, but message delays are unpredictable because of Internet traffic. *Wide area networks* and *local area networks* address the real-time problem of e-mail but the cost to set up the infrastructure and handle special accounts for those outside the team is prohibitive for most companies. *Electronic bulletin boards* can be used to supplement real-time communication, especially when communication involves multiple time zones three or more hours apart. An organization must plan to be flexible in the use of communication methods—EBBs, telephone conferences, faxes, e-mail, and so on.

Cultural and time-zone differences can affect the way a message is sent and received and the action taken. Team members should acquaint themselves with differences in communication to avoid misunderstandings.

To organize communications, invest in groupware packages to help the team manage the volume of e-mail. Standard groupware packages also permit a good measure of security. Consider using additional measures, such as encryption, for electronic and video communication outside the physical facility.

Bibliography

[1] J. Lipnack and J. Stamps, *Virtual Teams: Reaching Across Space, Time and Organizations With Technology*, Wiley & Sons, New York, 1997.

[2] S.P. Dunung, *Doing Business in Asia: The Complete Guide*, The Free Press, New York, 1994.

[3] L.W. Tuller, *Doing Business in Latin America & the Caribbean: Including Mexico, the U.S. Virgin Islands & Puerto Rico, Central America, South America*, AMACOM, New York, 1993.

[4] M. Johnson and R.T. Moran, *Cultural Guide to Doing Business in Europe*, Butterworth-Heinemann, Oxford, UK, 1992.

[5] P. Kenna and S. Lacy, *Business Japan: A Practical Guide to Understanding Japanese Business Culture*, NTC Publishing Group, Sumas, Wash., 1994.

[6] K.B. Bucknall, *Cultural Guide to Doing Business in China*, Butterworth-Heinemann, Oxford, UK, 1994.

[7] M. Hills, *Intranet as Groupware*, Wiley & Sons, New York, 1996.

[8] J. Woodcock, *Understanding Groupware in the Enterprise*, Microsoft Press, Redmond, Wash., 1997.

[9] A. Bacard, *The Computer Privacy Handbook: A Practical Guide to E-Mail Encryption, Data Protection, and PGP Privacy Software*, Peachpit Press, Berkeley, Calif., 1995.

[10] K. Birman, *Building Secure and Reliable Network Applications*, Prentice Hall, Upper Saddle River, N.J., 1997.

7

Managing the Pieces

Many virtual software development projects have been successfully launched, only to fall apart in their day-to-day management. The greatest challenge is to skillfully pull together the various pieces of the project in remote locations. The nature of a virtual project poses special challenges in risk management, the handling of cultural differences, project organization, software configuration management, and decision-making.

Risks

Risks are part of any project. Some believe that software projects have more risks than other types of projects because of the product's intangible nature, the diversity of methods used, and the types of people that typically make up a project team [1]. In general, the risks in a virtual project tend to be more centered around issues that are not completely visible, or issues that are not always communicated in a timely way.

Risks fall into three main categories. These are similar to risks for a nonvirtual project, but in a virtual project, they are amplified:

- *Organizational.* These pertain to the roles and responsibilities of the project participants. All team members must be aware of their tasks and any associated limitations. Examples of risks include not understanding who has the authority to make decisions, duplicating effort, and tasks being dropped because no one had a clear understanding of who was supposed to do what.

- *Technical.* These involve the methods and tools used to solve technical problems, such as improving the product's performance and the execution of development procedures. Risks include the misuse of the development methodology, inappropriate architecture selection, and the inability to integrate various subsections.

- *Communication.* These involve the technical infrastructure team members use to communicate with each other. Risks include misinterpreting discussions, inadequately communicating ideas and expectations, and having a communication medium that is unacceptably slow.

As Figure 7.1 shows, the three areas overlap. Thus, the overlaps represent risks from multiple areas. In prioritizing risk mitigation plans, these overlaps should be first on the list.

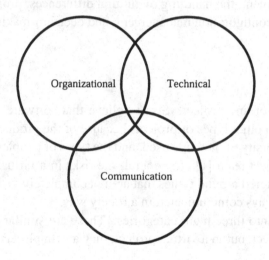

Figure 7.1: Major risks for global software development.

Cultural Differences

In Chapters 5 and 6, I touched on how cultural differences affect accountability and communications, respectively, and suggested that the team research the cultures represented in the project. In this chapter, I offer several suggestions for directing that research to aid in revealing a culture's business expectations. Again, several good books can tell you what to observe when doing business in other countries [2, 3, 4, 5, 6].

- *Find out how families and communities are structured.* In most instances, business expectations are carried over from the cultural aspects of how a family and community behave. For example, in Japan workers tend to put in long hours with little time for their families. In most European countries, on the other hand, it is common practice to stop work as soon as the normal day is over (regardless of what stage the work is in) and go home.

- *Read up on the history of the culture.* You may avoid communication and behavioral problems if you know how certain cultures feel about others. Much interaction is not based solely on performance, but on predetermined attitudes, which often go back generations. For example, on one project, I observed two normally polite and open people become visibly heated and distrustful during a controversial conversation about the direction of their work group. Another team member pointed out that each was from an ethnic group that had fought each other for centuries. Putting these individuals in the same group was not a good idea.

- *Find ex-patriots of the representative countries.* Consultants or students can provide insights into the problems of managing people associated with their culture. Living in a different country often brings such people new perspectives on their native culture, its unique features, and how it differs from the culture in which they're living now. These people can be invaluable resources of information about cultural backgrounds that drive attitudes toward delegation, control, work-family relationships, holidays, and so on.

Organization

As I mentioned in Chapter 2, there are many ways to organize a virtual team. Regardless of what method you choose, you should follow the same rules you would to build any strong management team:

- *Put people others respect and trust in management positions.* Good people will overcome technical, administrative, cultural, and other issues.

- *Keep the structure simple and communicate it well.* People in a virtual environment will be anxious about being a part of an organization because they are not in daily face-to-face contact. There are likely to be both shared and individual responsibilities. Make it clear which is which and communicate individual accountability. I describe this in more detail later. As I covered in Chapter 3, a software development plan that identifies processes and responsibilities provides a common document for the entire virtual team.

- *Assign leaders who are not afraid to travel.* This seems obvious, but I have seen project leaders who have a fear of flying or going to unfamiliar places. These individuals are not a good choice for leadership because many issues are best resolved face to face. If the leader can't travel, the travel hardship then falls on the other members of the team. This may be problematic if the software has been outsourced to a different company. At the very least, the rest of the team at that location must pick up the leader's travel obligations, which can foster resentment.

Software Configuration Management

As I mentioned in Chapter 5, SCM is key to controlling the many pieces of a virtual project. The virtual SCM board, like most SCM boards, must perform several important tasks in a timely manner:

- *Represent all affected and interested functional and organizational parties.* This means bringing up all sides of an issue and seeking input from parties that may not be present during a meeting.

- *Review, approve, or reject proposed changes to the software.* This includes version control and making sure that changing one function will not negatively affect the others.

- *Ensure that the proper process and documentation exists.* Documentation control is critical to the smooth functioning of a virtual project. All decisions and their rationale must be documented and communicated to all members of the team.

The SCM board for a distributed project differs from the traditional SCM board because it must do these functions from remote locations, as Figure 7.2b shows.

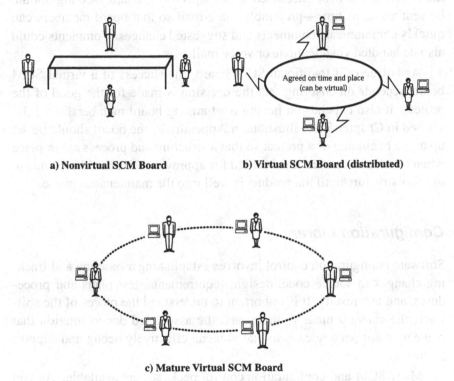

a) Nonvirtual SCM Board   b) Virtual SCM Board (distributed)

c) Mature Virtual SCM Board

Figure 7.2: Nonvirtual versus virtual software configuration management boards.

In Figure 7.2a, the board meets in a central physical location. In Figure 7.2b, the board uses either telephone or videoconferencing to conduct meetings at a prearranged time. In Figure 7.2c, the CM support functions, such as libraries are centralized, but serve a virtual team; that is, there is no specified place and time for interaction.

Figure 7.2c represents a more mature virtual SCM board. Here, the board functions by reviewing material and approving or disapproving requests on packages received electronically. Normally, each SCM board request has a deadline by which to respond instead of a common meeting time, as in traditional SCM boards (this practice is also acceptable when meeting in a chat room or video conference).

To ensure the virtual SCM board runs efficiently, agenda and reference materials that will be discussed at the upcoming board meeting should be sent ahead of time—preferably via e-mail so that board members can quickly communicate comments and suggested changes. Comments could also be handled via telephone or voice mail.

As is true of a traditional SCM board, the success of a virtual SCM board depends on ensuring that the decision is made for the good of the project. It also depends on having trust among board members. As I described in Chapter 5 and illustrate in Appendix B, the board should be set up at the beginning of a project so that a structure and process are in place when the first document is submitted for approval. You should continue to use this structure until the product is well into the maintenance phase.

Configuration Library

Software configuration control involves establishing a baseline and tracking changes to source code, design, requirements, test plans and procedures, and test results. It is important to understand the pieces of the software, the changes made to them, and the associated documentation that make up a software release so that you can effectively debug and support it later on.

Many SCM and configuration control packages are available. As you start your project, you should have compatible configuration control software at each remote location. You should also set up a central configuration control library, as shown in Figure 7.3.

In this illustration each remote area has a copy of its own configuration control software. During a planned interval (weekly is usually adequate), each area sends updates to the central library. From the central library, software builds are made for testing and eventually for the product.

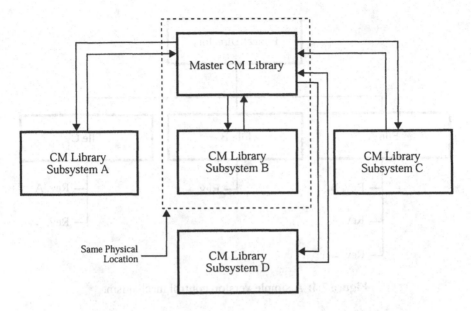

Figure 7.3: A centralized configuration control library.

Version Control

Version control is the discipline of documenting changes and storing them. It offers several key benefits:

- It identifies the exact configuration of each source code and documentation source file used for testing and in the product.

- It lets developers attach notes to the software compiled, such as date, development environment, and test plan identifiers.

- It allows controls, such as read and write privileges, to individuals and groups.

- It provides change history if access is needed to an earlier revision.

For small, simple projects, a directory and file system, such as that illustrated in Figure 7.4, is an adequate version control mechanism. In this figure, a directory is set up for the project. Each file in the project has its own subdirectory with copies of the files that make up its revision history.

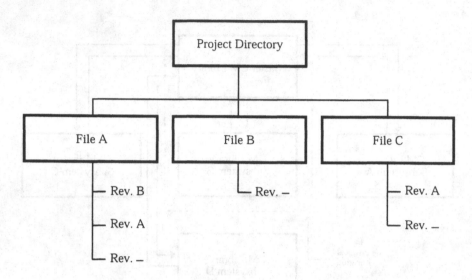

Figure 7.4: A simple version control mechanism.

Most projects should use a commercial version control system to let multiple users track their own file histories as well as to tie individual file versions to a total project configuration. Ronald Berlack provides additional information on version control systems and SCM concepts [7].

Figure 7.5 shows an implementation of a version control system for a virtual environment. Similar to the central library concept described in the last section, the figure shows a version control system for each developer at a remote location with updates going to a central control system for the entire project. The central version control system handles updates automatically and tracks changes to the various files.

Documentation Control

Documentation control is another important SCM task. A virtual organization requires more documentation control than other types of organizational structures because key people may be hard to access.

Under normal business conditions, misunderstandings about decisions and policies are common. This is magnified in a virtual environment, where access to people who can provide clarification and more detail is

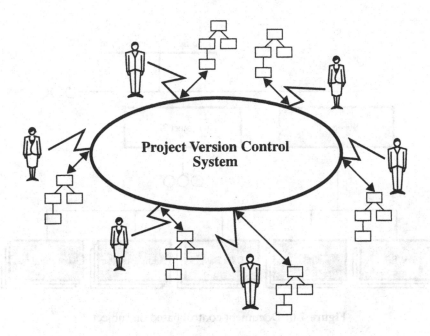

Figure 7.5: Version control system in a virtual environment.

difficult [8]. To minimize these misunderstandings, a documentation trail is needed.

Documentation control can take different forms. As a minimum, a project folder should be created and maintained. Figure 7.6 shows an organization by subject area. In this approach, documents are organized by various subjects and then could be further subdivided by date and/or originator.

Another way to organize a document control system is by originator, as shown in Figure 7.7. In this approach, the emphasis is not placed on subject areas but on historical files and on correspondence from the people who generated the text.

Document control based on subject works best in larger projects, while smaller projects are a better match for document control based on originator. A relational database engine that links references to subject and author will give you the flexibility to combine the two approaches, accessing documents by both subject and originator.

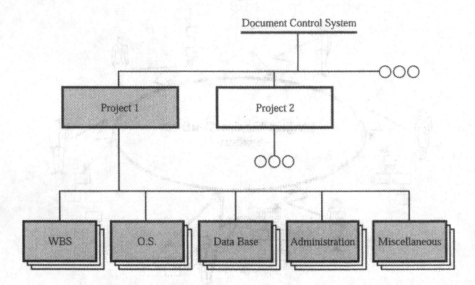

Figure 7.6: Document control based on subject.

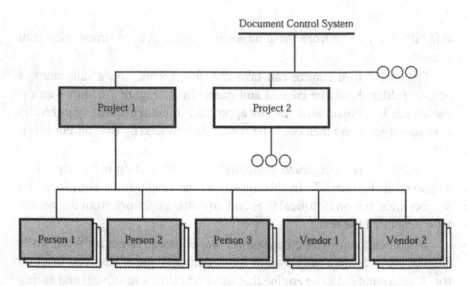

Figure 7.7: Document control based on the document originator.

Implementing a document control system requires more discipline than complicated software tools. The originator of the document must electronically file a copy under document control or send a copy to a document control administrator who then files it under the project's document control system. To ensure that people follow this process rigorously, management should institutionalize the practice through approved processes or procedures.

Decision Making and Accountability

In a virtual team environment distributed decision making should be encouraged. A centralized decision-making policy will slow development and reduce the morale of the members not at the central development location. Like most projects, different views and opinions will be voiced and will be raised in the project structure. There should be some mechanism to resolve these differences, from both a technical and business perspective.

As I described in Chapter 5, the design authority is the person designated to resolve technical differences. This person has the final say on differences of options, implementation, and test strategy and on performance tradeoffs. The design authority may be the chief engineer or project manager. Whoever the person, he should be identified before the project, since many issues involving the conceptual approach will require tradeoffs that the design authority should direct.

The business authority should address conflicts relating to budget, schedule, resources, markets, and customers. In larger virtual projects, many managers will make these types of decisions for their pieces of the project. The business authority will have the final accountability on tradeoffs and issues relating to the assurance that the project meets its business commitments.

Key Thoughts

The greatest challenge is to skillfully pull together the various pieces of the project in remote locations. This involves looking at sources of technical, organizational, and communication risk. Cultural differences will also determine how you manage parts of the project. It is important to understand what drives a culture emotionally and socially.

In organizing the project, assign people others respect and trust as managers and be sure they are not afraid to travel. Keep the project structure as simple as possible and clearly communicate lines of responsibility.

Software configuration management is key in holding a virtual project together. The virtual SCM board must represent all affected and interested functional and organizational parties; review, approve, or reject proposed changes to the software; and ensure that the proper process and documentation exists. A centralized configuration library helps in configuration control. A version control system helps track changes. A simple directory and file system will suffice in small projects. A centralized version control system should automatically handle changes from each remote site. Documentation control is also important. Systems based on subject work better for larger projects; systems based on originator work better for smaller ones.

Distributed decision-making should be encouraged, but there should be some mechanism to resolve differences, both from a technical and business perspective. The design authority, typically the project manager or chief engineer, should handle technical conflicts, while the business manager should help mediate conflicts like budget, schedule, and resources.

Bibliography

[1] D. Karolak, *Software Engineering Risk Management*, IEEE CS Press, Los Alamitos, Calif., 1996.

[2] S.P. Dunung, *Doing Business in Asia: The Complete Guide*, The Free Press, New York, 1994.

[3] L.W. Tuller, *Doing Business in Latin America & the Caribbean: Including Mexico, the U.S. Virgin Islands & Puerto Rico, Central America, South America*, AMACOM, New York, 1993.

[4] M. Johnson and R.T. Moran, *Cultural Guide to Doing Business in Europe*, Butterworth-Heinemann, Oxford, UK, 1992.

[5] P. Kenna and S. Lacy, *Business Japan: A Practical Guide to Understanding Japanese Business Culture*, NTC Publishing Group, Sumas, Wash., 1994.

[6] K.B. Bucknall, *Cultural Guide to Doing Business in China*, Butterworth-Heinemann, Oxford, UK, 1994.

[7] R. Berlack, *Software Configuration Management*, Wiley & Sons, New York, 1991.

[8] R. Maruca, "How Do You Manage an Off-Site Team?" *Harvard Business Review*, Vol. 76, July–Aug. 1998, pp. 22–35.

8

Integration

At this point in the global project, the virtual team should have workable communication methods, be following the software configuration management plan, and be using a common set of tools. As a manager, you have guided the team as they selected an architecture and developed a software plan. You continue to encourage them to work through cultural differences and divide tasks to ensure productivity across multiple time zones.

It would seem that the hard work is over, but it's not. One of the most difficult parts of any software development project is integration—whether it's integrating software pieces, integrating software and new hardware, or some of both. In a virtual environment, integration becomes more difficult because you may not have access to all the resources you need for problem-solving during this phase.

As in many activities I've described in this book, integration planning starts well before integration begins. It involves creating an integration strategy, acquiring the right kind of tools, writing or using commercial test suites, determining acceptance criteria, creating documentation, and providing the right level of support. The management milestone chart in Appendix B shows where in the development life cycle integration activities begin and key points in the integration process.

Strategies

If not properly planned, integration in a global virtual environment will yield myriad pieces of software—all at various levels of completeness in testing and documentation. Even worse, different versions of the software will be sent to the virtual locations. A solid integration strategy can help avoid this nightmare. There are three possibilities, which Figure 8.1 illustrates.

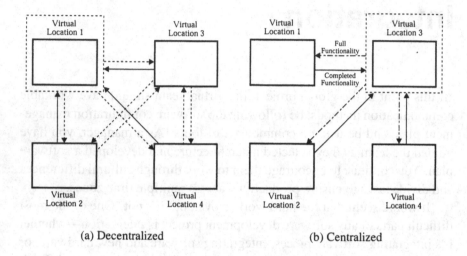

(a) Decentralized   (b) Centralized

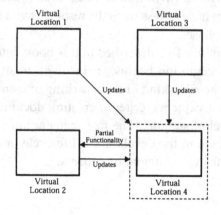

(c) Just-in-Time

Figure 8.1: Software integration strategies.

Decentralized

In Figure 8.1a, software is being developed at Virtual Location 1, which is also the site where a subsystem is being developed. Virtual Locations 2, 3, and 4 transmit a copy of their software to Virtual Location 1, which integrates what it receives and tests it with the rest of the application. Likewise, Virtual Location 1 transmits its software to Virtual Locations 2, 3, and 4, which also integrate what they receive and test it.

The advantage of this strategy is that each site receives the latest version of the developed software. The disadvantage is that the version received may contain unexpected errors because work is still in progress as testing continues and each site gets its results. This strategy works best when the project team is small and the development cycle is short.

Centralized

In Figure 8.1b, each virtual location sends a copy of its software to Virtual Location 3, where a central integration library is kept. In the figure, each location, as shown in Virtual Location 1 is taking a snapshot of the centralized version.

The advantage of this strategy is that there is less effort debugging the software because it is submitted under configuration control for integration. That is, it is not a work in progress, as in the decentralized integration strategy, but has completed all testing. This means it must have either zero or at least a very few compilation errors. The disadvantage of this strategy is that the centralized library will populate more slowly because it will take longer for the software to meet the rules of clean compilation with full functionality, and so on, than in a decentralized strategy.

The centralized strategy works best when the development cycle is long and only a few parts of the software are changing.

Just-in-Time

Here integration is based on incremental builds [1]. In Figure 8.1c, partial functionality is sent to a centralized location—in this case, Virtual Location 4. This strategy also requires a central integration library. At different times during integration, functionality is added to the library. To test a function in Virtual Location 2, the developers at that location download a copy of the baseline for testing. As functionality is added, other virtual locations update the centralized location with software that has limited, instead of complete, functionality.

The advantage of this strategy is that it provides a controlled library with few errors, as in the centralized strategy, but without the long wait for a complete functional system. That is, because limited functionality is added incrementally, development and integration can be continuous. The disadvantage is that the telecommunications method may not be able to handle the potentially large volume of data. Also, this strategy requires more management attention to change control when the software gets into the library because there will be many incremental submissions.

The just-in-time strategy works best when projects are designed and implemented function-by-function over a short development life cycle.

Tools

Tools are important during integration because they act on code that reflects the project team's first attempt to produce a tangible product. Tools for successful virtual integration fall into three general categories:

- *Software configuration management.* SCM tools, as described in Chapter 7, are used to trace and manage software versions during development. This includes software in all locations. In addition to typical SCM capabilities, the SCM system must support distributed software development. For example, it must be able to accept files from outside its host environment.

- *Integration.* Integration tools bring the various pieces of software together. They have three major capabilities: they can build software releases with errors and incomplete software modules; they can resolve undefined references; and they offer the opportunity to bring in previous versions of individual software modules via the linker. Integration tools used in a virtual project are the same as those for local development except that the virtual tools must be able to retrieve software outside the local development environment. For example, they should be able to patch in unresolved references that arise when the outside software to be integrated provides incomplete information.

- *Debugging.* Debugging tools must be able to address multiple modules and modules between development environments. In addition to the attributes of most debugging tools, debugging tools for integration should include source debugging across modules and multiple windows for viewing code and memory.

Test Suites

Testing is an integral part of integration because it establishes a baseline functionality that meets the software's design and requirements. Test suites provide a documented means of verifying what software was tested (and not tested) and how.

You should develop two types of test suites—one for the software developed at the local site and one for the complete system. Figure 8.2 illustrates.

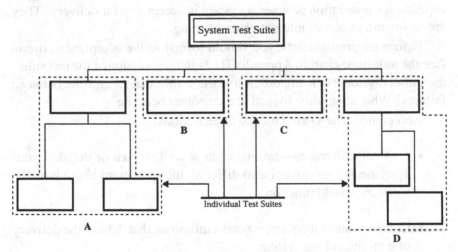

Figure 8.2: System (double box) and individual (dotted boxes) test suites.

In the figure, site test suites are denoted by dotted boxes. The system test suite is denoted by the double box at the top of the figure. This test suite is not a collection of individual test suites, but instead reflects the system's functionality and should be traceable to the system requirements.

Test suites let the developer identify the test strategies, methods, environment, and functionality to be tested. Once documented and automated, the test suites provide a baseline for future enhancement and regression testing when the software changes. As such, they should be put under configuration control.

Acceptance Criteria

Virtual projects face the same problems as large nonvirtual projects, including how to merge many pieces of software. In a large development environment, you may face issues such as who should have found the integration problem and who is liable to fix it if the software ready for integration does not meet the design specifications. Acceptance criteria are the list of requirements for determining when a subsection of software is acceptable for integration or when a system is acceptable for delivery. They are an important part of integration and testing.

Before integration starts, you should formalize the acceptance criteria (see the milestone chart in Appendix B). Is the completion of the test suites the only criterion? Is it important to meet a minimal mean time between failures? What about time logged at a customer beta site?

Acceptance criteria are vital for three reasons:

- Cultural differences—no matter how well-written or detailed your agreements are—give rise to differing interpretations about how the software should function.

- Contracts and subcontracts need a milestone that defines the delivery of a product or subsystem.

- There should be no, or at least very few, shades of gray in determining whether the software meets requirements.

Even the most basic acceptance criteria should define the system's minimal functionality down to the module level. The traceability matrix (described later) helps here. Software developers then know which function to develop, test, and integrate first.

Acceptance criteria can also identify behavioral and nonbehavioral requirements. Figure 8.3 shows the relationship of acceptance criteria to requirements, code, and test plans and procedures. Because acceptance criteria require traceability and are applied in the later phases of the development life cycle, they are usually associated with testing.

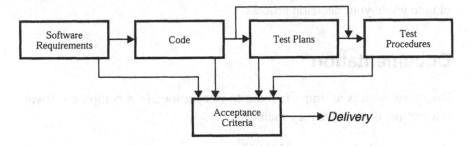

Figure 8.3: Acceptance criteria associations.

In the figure, software requirements are used as a basis to establish the software's functionality. How the functionality is implemented in the code and the software behavior are also inputs into creating the acceptance criteria. Test plans and procedures deal with how the software responds to the user environment and how it acts under certain stress conditions.

In most deliveries, the acceptance criteria also depend on:

- *Customer/market expectations.* These may have changed since requirements were specified.

- *Amount of time.* Time pressures may have dictated a sacrifice in functionality. Likewise, relaxing the time constraint may have provided the opportunity to increase functionality.

- *Available funds.* As in the time criterion, functionality may have decreased or increased with the corresponding change in funds.

- *State of the software.* Aspects of this criterion include required functionality (does the software have the required functions?) and number of errors (are the errors within what the customer will accept as a first release?).

You will always make tradeoffs among these kinds of influences. There is no magic combination for all projects. Acceptance criteria simply give you a plan. By identifying the factors that play into a particular acceptance criterion, you are in essence documenting an acceptance process. When the pressure is on to make an acceptance decision, at least you'll have a plan to guide your decision process.

Documentation

Documentation is an important aid to integration. In a complex software integration, documents may include:

- *Traceability matrix.* Identifies the functions the software should meet and what module meets them. This contrasts to first identifying the software modules and then the function. Figure 8.4 shows a sample matrix.

- *Description of the integration environment.* Describes the tools, process, and version of test suites, test configuration files, and the like used in integration testing. This document provides a reference for regression testing and debugging once the software has been released. In many cases, rebuilding a release to re-create a problem the customer has identified is important in problem solving.

- *Module version matrix.* Identifies each software module and the configuration version used in an integration build. Figure 8.5 shows a sample matrix. This matrix type can be found in a linker and/or in SCM systems.

Chapter 7 identifies other types of documents, correspondence, and notes that extend to the integration phase.

Function Number	Function Name	Source	Software Module(s)	Comments
1	Update Query	Paragraph 4.3.2 of user requirements	Get prompt Process-query	Version 4.1 updated with this function
2	Graph Plots	Paragraph 1.7.2.1 and paragraph 5.4 of user requirements	Process-graphs, Plot-graphs	New requirement added
3	Format Protocols	Paragraph 1.8 of Software Requirements Specifications	Format protocol-output	Internal requirement

Figure 8.4: Example of a traceability matrix.

Virtual Support

Not many integration efforts succeed without adequate support. This is doubly true for virtual environments. As I described in Chapters 6 and 7, development and communication tools and an infrastructure that accommodates different time zones will make integration go more smoothly. Specific support tools for integration include an e-mail system; a Web site that contains a depository for text, code, and test results; voice mail; and copies of tools for individual virtual locations to use in development and testing.

Communications and a means to express textual information as completely as possible are key to virtual integration support. Supplementing textual information with voice contact further clarifies problems and provides additional information. As with most problem-solving activities, direct and timely access to a live individual is the best communication method. As I mentioned in Chapter 2, you should have some organization documentation to identify individuals. As I discussed in Chapter 5, technical problems are typically resolved through design authorities.

Key Thoughts

One of the most difficult parts of any software development project is integration. In a virtual environment, integration becomes more difficult because you may not have access to all the resources you need for problem-solving and to make the total integration process visible. An integration strategy is essential. Integration can be decentralized, centralized, or just-in-time. The *decentralized* approach, in which software pieces are sent

Module Name	Version	Date
Index-Value	3.2	15-09-98
Process Image	1.1.2	24-02-98
Delete Process	4.2.7	13-11-97
Initiate Task	2.0	05-01-98
.	.	.
.	.	.
.	.	.

Figure 8.5: Example of a module version matrix.

out without complete testing, works best when the project involves a small group and a short development cycle. The *centralized* approach, in which one location handles integration using a central library, works best when the development cycle is long and only a few parts of the software are changing. The *just-in-time* approach, in which functionality is added to a central library in increments, works best when projects are designed and implemented by function over a short development life cycle.

Adequate integration tools are also important. You should aim to have software configuration management tools that support distributed software development, integration tools that can retrieve software outside the local development environment, and debugging tools that provide source debugging across modules and multiple windows for viewing code and memory.

Testing is part of any integration. You should develop two types of test suites—one for the software developed at each site and one for the entire system.

Acceptance criteria are an important part of integration and testing. They tell everyone how to determine when a subsection of software is acceptable for integration or when a system is acceptable for delivery. At the very least they should define the system's minimal functionality down to the module level.

Documents help unify expectations during integration. Basic documents include a traceability matrix, which identifies the functions the software should meet and what module meets them; a description of the integration environment, including supporting tools; and a module version matrix, which identifies each software module and the configuration version used in an integration build.

Integration must be adequately supported with communication methods and infrastructures, such as e-mail, voice mail, and Web sites that contain copies of a virtual location's tools.

Bibliography

[1] D. Karolak, *Software Engineering Risk Management*, IEEE CS Press, Los Alamitos, Calif., 1996.

9
Maintenance

Developing software in a virtual environment should be challenge enough, but issues continue into maintenance. Not only will you face problems typical of any large software development, such as who is responsible for maintaining what, but you will also face obstacles stemming from cultural differences.

In most cases, the virtual team is focused on meeting schedule and quality issues before releasing the software to the customer. Maintenance planning tends to be overlooked, which means maintenance becomes an afterthought. The only problem with that approach is that when you hit the maintenance phase, there is no support environment or personnel in place—and critical documents, such as design rationale, may no longer be accessible.

Thinking out maintenance activities before they are needed is essential [1, 2]. As the milestone chart in Appendix B indicates, you should begin maintenance planning very early in the project. A good maintenance plan starts with understanding and reconciling cultural differences that can work against effective maintenance. It also includes selecting an appropriate maintenance model and establishing an effective maintenance environment. Finally, maintenance always involves evaluating tradeoffs between continuing with the current set of development tools or investing in upgrades.

Cultural Differences

As in other activities of a virtual project, cultural differences, if not properly addressed, can sabotage a project, or at least make it very difficult to run. Managers of virtual projects tend not to see subtle attitudes that can influence the way business is conducted, and maintenance is no exception.

For example, cultures differ on the length and assignment of maintenance staff and in what constitutes quality customer support.

In project staffing, the attitude of most US software developers and managers is to move resources to the next project soon after, or even before delivering the current product. This may pose problems for maintenance because it can delay the responsiveness to customer requests. Those in the Far East culture, on the other hand, tend to keep a larger team of developers longer after delivery to work on quality issues. Thus, their response to initial customer requests is very organized and fairly rapid.

Cultures also differ on how much support they consider adequate. In North American culture, long-term support may take a back seat to the company's need to open new markets. In Japanese culture, quality and customer satisfaction are key, so much emphasis is placed on long-term support. Support is also important in India's culture. In Europe, support as it relates to customer satisfaction is mixed. Countries that tend to be more pragmatic in their business practices, such as the United Kingdom, may adopt a "you get what you pay for" policy about support. Other countries, such as Italy, focus more on customer satisfaction beyond signed business agreements.

Maintenance Models

One of the goals of a maintenance model is to settle who is responsible for fixing what. As the milestone chart in Appendix B shows, the virtual team sets up the maintenance model during contractual arrangements. This may seem unnecessarily early, but unless it is done at this stage, the needed resources—tools and personnel—will either be underused (and thus wasted) or strained to inefficiency when the work begins. Worse, there will be no infrastructure, and maintenance activities will degenerate into managing a string of crises. Response to the customer—the whole point of maintenance—will be delayed. I once observed a team that was so focused on development and the product delivery date that they did not plan maintenance until shortly after the first delivery. When problems and the need for updates were identified, the company had a hard time finding experienced people, who for lack of planning, had gone on to other projects. The maintainers they finally did draft faced many obstacles, including incomplete or missing documentation that often did not match the source code or test results. Getting time with the experienced people to document their experience was difficult. Finding undocumented "homegrown" tools was difficult and changing them was impossible. Undocumented process steps, such as changes in the manual linker address or special test steps, came as a surprise. Consequently, it took an extraordinarily long time to add features and correct problems in the early release. This in turn caused customers to feel abandoned and undermined customer goodwill and confidence. All this could have been avoided had the team settled on a maintenance model much earlier and thus had the resources they needed.

Maintenance models that work for virtual development include distributed, centralized, and single.

Distributed

Figure 9.1 shows the *distributed* approach, in which each part of the virtual organization is responsible for issues regarding product performance or quality. The review board, which contains representatives from each development organization, is responsible for verifying the problem, assessing which parts of the software are affected, and providing all the relevant software development organizations information to resolve the problem. Part of the information sent to the development organizations should include the problem report, conditions under which the problem occurred, the software release/configuration information, and other known problems and their solutions.

Information received from the software development organizations includes updated source code; design documentation (if applicable); test procedures and test results; and information about the solution and test environment, such as the compiler and linker versions, test tool versions, and a description of the test environment.

Centralized

Figure 9.2 shows a *centralized* maintenance model, in which a separate autonomous organization is created to maintain the software after its deliv-

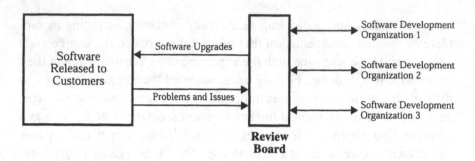

Figure 9.1: Distributed software maintenance model.

ery. The autonomous organization handles problems from customers and the delivery of any upgrades. This organization is usually funded by all the development organizations in the virtual organization; it may also be a separate legal entity with its own revenue responsibilities. The activities performed are generally the same as those performed in the distributed maintenance model.

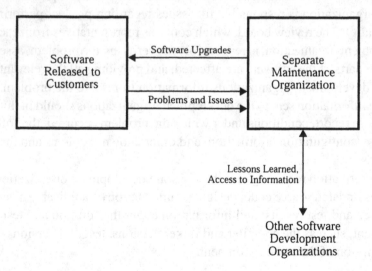

Figure 9.2: Centralized maintenance model.

The autonomous organization is usually staffed with representatives from the various member development organizations, who are transferred to the new structure. Each organization contributes some to the history and knowledge of the software, as well as providing access to the source code—all of which works to bring the organization up to its full capacity very rapidly.

Single

Figure 9.3 shows the *single* maintenance model, in which one of the software development organizations assumes maintenance responsibilities for the entire virtual organization. As in the centralized model, the organization inherits the software configuration library, tools, and so on to provide a solid base of knowledge about and access to the software.

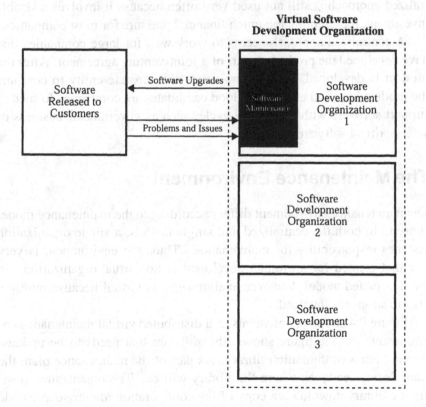

Figure 9.3: A single maintenance approach.

Which Is Best?

For a virtual project with many small organizations, the distributed model may work best. If one of the organizations has a sufficient infrastructure in place, the single model may make more sense.

When companies are global, the single model seems to be the most successful, although the maintaining organization will go through a longer learning curve to support problem solving outside its original development scope. The distributed approach often gives rise to responsiveness problems because it requires better coordination and communication between various parties. A problem may be given to the wrong party to fix and then passed around until the right party can be found to fix it. The centralized approach is still not used very often because it involves a sizable investment, representing too much financial pressure for most companies.

A centralized approach seems to work well for large companies that have developed the product as part of a joint-venture agreement. After the product is developed, the partners create the separate entity to continue the product base and expand it. Good candidates are companies formed to support software with a long life cycle, such as government, business or safety-critical software.

The Maintenance Environment

The maintenance environment differs according to the maintenance model chosen. In both the centralized and single models, a single organization assumes responsibility for maintenance. Thus, the environment is very like that created for a product developed in nonvirtual organization. In the distributed model, however, maintenance is virtual because multiple organizations are involved.

Figure 9.4 shows the elements of a distributed virtual maintenance environment. As the figure shows, the software that needs to be updated comes from a configuration library. As part of the maintenance plan, the team decides early on where the library will be. The organization hosting the library downloads a copy of the configuration master source code along with the executable code for the rest of the system from other member companies in the virtual organization. Once they update the software

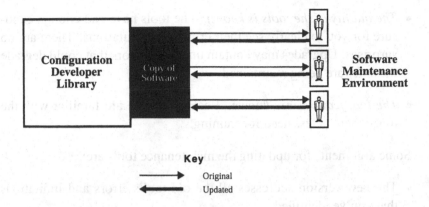

Figure 9.4: Distributed virtual software maintenance environment.

being maintained and verify it, the remote organizations link it in with the copy of the executable software system in the central library.

Besides updating source code, the maintaining organizations need to check test procedures and scripts, user documentation, and so on to see if the changes in the software affect how it is tested and how the user uses it. These other parts of the support environment and deliverables are often overlooked, yet they must be maintained to ensure that current and future changes are tested properly.

Once the maintaining organization tests the source code change in the system and performs a regression test, it upgrades the test environment (test scripts, documentation, compiler, liner, editor, and so on) and user manuals. It then checks all these items back into the configuration library for use in future updates.

Updating Development Tools

When the software is delivered to the customer, a copy of the development environment, including development tools, should be stored under configuration control. At some point you may want to upgrade those tools as new versions become available.

The arguments for keeping the existing version are:

- *The quality of the tools is known.* The tools have had enough exposure for you to clearly see their errors and limitations. There are no surprises. Upgrades may contain unknown errors that could degrade the software being maintained.

- *The tool features are known.* Because people are familiar with the tools, there is less need for training.

Some arguments for updating the maintenance tools are:

- The new version addresses all the old tool's errors and limitations that you've identified.

- The new version has features that may be more useful in maintaining the software.

- The software vendor may no longer support the existing tool version.

A major factor in deciding whether to keep the existing version of the tools is the amount of time the product will be supported. If the product is expected to have a short maintenance life, keep the current version. Likewise, the longer the maintenance activity, the larger the investment in upgrading and testing software tools.

Key Thoughts

Not only will you face problems typical of any large software development, such as who is responsible for maintaining what, but you will also face obstacles stemming from cultural differences. These include attitudes about staffing and what constitutes quality customer support.

Successful virtual maintenance depends on establishing a maintenance model early in the project so that everyone agrees on who should handle problems after the product is delivered. In the *distributed* maintenance model, each part of the virtual organization is responsible for issues regarding performance or quality related to the software it produced. The review board, which contains representatives from each development organization, is responsible for verifying the problem, assessing which parts of the software are affected, and providing the software development organizations information to resolve the problem. In the *centralized* model, a separate autonomous organization is created to maintain the software after its delivery. Finally, in the *single* model, one of the development organizations in the virtual organization is selected to be solely responsible for all maintenance.

For a virtual project with many small organizations, the distributed model may work best. When companies are global or when one company is large enough to have an infrastructure in place, the single model may be preferable. A centralized approach seems to work well for large companies that have developed the product as part of a joint-venture agreement.

Virtual maintenance, which occurs with the distributed maintenance model, must have a suitable environment. Besides updating the source code through a local or remote configuration library, the maintaining organization must check test procedures and scripts, user documentation, and so on to see if the changes in the software affect how it is tested and how the user uses it. All these items are then checked backed into the configuration library for use in future updates.

At some point, the maintaining organization may want to update the maintenance tools, which involves certain tradeoffs. On the one hand, the team knows the tools' limitations and features. There are no surprises. On the other hand, the new version may contain features that enhance maintenance in some way. Generally, in a short maintenance phase, it's more economical to keep the existing tools. Longer term, larger developments generally require more investment in tool updates.

Bibliography

[1] *IEEE-Std.-1219, IEEE Standard for Software Maintenance*, IEEE CS Press, Los Alamitos, Calif., 1992.

[2] T.M. Pigoski, *Practical Software Maintenance: Best Practices for Managing Your Software Investment*, John Wiley & Sons, New York, 1996.

10
Three Case Studies

Thus far, I've covered virtual software teams, strategic partnering, out-sourcing, cultural differences, responsibility and accountability, cost struc-tures, and configuration management. Yet, successfully managing a virtual project requires that you look beyond these concepts in isolation. You must also understand how they interrelate. To that end, I present three case stud-ies: a small software company in a strategic alliance with an Asian com-pany, a large corporation that puts two divisions divided by an ocean on the same software project, and a company who outsources a software sub-system overseas. Although these companies are fictitious, they are fairly representative of companies I've heard about and worked with. You may have already encountered some of these challenges in your own projects.

Webmaster Inc.

Webmaster is a small company only five years old. In the last three years, its sales have doubled each year. Webmaster began by doing local Web and Internet development and grew to provide service on a national level. Its success thus far had been bringing companies on-board with inter- and intranet Web pages and software support.

The Arrangement

Last year, WQW, a Japanese software company with $200 million in sales, contacted the Webmaster's president expressing interest in an arrangement that would help WQW put its interactive game software on the Web. For Webmaster, this was an opportunity to diversify and gain knowledge in interactive graphics; for WQW, it represented entry into the Web market and a chance to gain Internet expertise.

After several months of exploring potential business relationships, the companies decided to form a strategic alliance. The companies felt that such an alliance would allow them to benefit from each other's technology without forcing them to be competitors in the same market segment.

The Project

The first project under this strategic alliance, dubbed Red Spider, was to develop interactive PC games for multiple players on the Web by adapting an existing popular game. Three members from WQW and two members from Webmaster formed the project team.

The team decided to communicate in English because most developers at WQW learned English at the public school and university level and because none of the employees at Webmaster spoke any Japanese.

To communicate with team members at WQW and to control the project, Webmaster decided to set up a Web page that was password protected. Figure 10.1 shows the Web page organization. The Web page had entries for a communication bulletin board to announce items of mutual interest, a chat room for developers to meet for meetings, and an entry for documenting requirements, design, and test results. The Web page also contained entries for source-code control (who updated what piece and its status), project schedules, and a list of project members' names, phone numbers, and e-mail addresses.

As the project progressed, communications began to settle into a pattern. WQW team members would send e-mail as they were leaving, and the Webmaster team would read it as they came in that morning. Conference calls were scheduled in the evening when initiated by Webmaster or in the morning when initiated by WQW. The calls were limited to no more than two hours.

The Difficulties

During one conference call, a WQW engineer mentioned with evident pride, that they had filed for several patents on Web-based interactive graphic design, which were based on the work done in the last several months on Red Spider. Several engineers at Webmaster became upset,

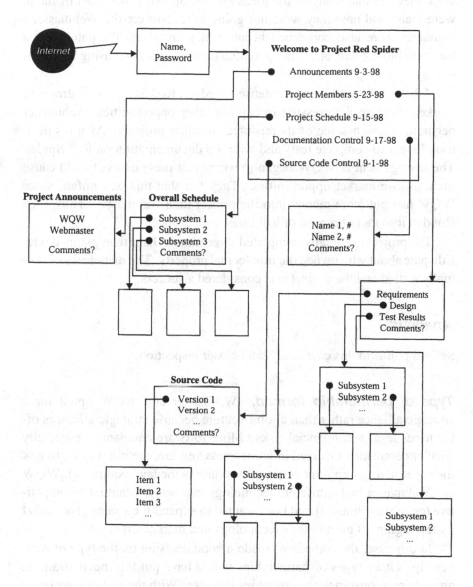

Figure 10.1: Organization of the Web page for the Red Spider project.

since they felt that many of the ideas on Red Spider, if not most of them, were theirs and now they were not going to receive credit. Webmaster's managers were also concerned because they could see the patents as a means to block them, and other potential competitors, from using this technology.

After nearly a year on an intense schedule, Red Spider was almost to market. Feeling the pressure to capture other opportunities, Webmaster began to reassign some of its resources to other projects. As a result, it took longer to complete tests and wrap up documentation on Red Spider. The management at WQW began to worry that these delays would cause them to lose market opportunities. They felt that this was unfair, since WQW had put more money into the project than Webmaster. Thus, they stood to lose more because of lost sales.

The project eventually completed three months later than planned with a dispute about who owned the intellectual property. The dispute was eventually settled and the project was considered a success.

Analysis

Several points in this case study bear closer inspection.

Type of partnership formed. Webmaster and WQW opted for a strategic alliance rather than a joint venture because strategic alliances offer fewer legal and financial risks. More software companies, especially smaller companies involved in an overseas venture, are not willing to risk the expense to set up joint corporations (unless the law requires it). WQW and Webmaster had a different technology that was not mutually competitive (or so they thought) and both wanted to expand their sales and market by leveraging off each other's technology and market structure.

In this case, the companies made a good decision on the type of partnership. Other types of partnerships would have put too much strain on an early relationship with companies this size. With the fast rate software technology turns over, long-term joint ventures for software development will occur less often. The changing technology and market competition will force different companies to work together for a shorter time.

Of course, the two companies did not escape without some consequence for inadequate legal planning, but first-time ventures are seldom perfect—a trend I hope this book can help change.

Lack of prior agreement about intellectual property ownership.
Neither Webmaster nor WQW thought to establish policy about who owned what intellectual property (see Appendix A). There was also no prior agreement on how intellectual property was to be managed. WQW took the initiative and filed patent disclosures on new inventions addressing the use of high-resolution graphics and Web technology. This put Webmaster in the difficult position of negotiating to protect its investment and future market based on innovations made during Red Spider. The two companies needed to sit down and hash out a course of action acceptable to both. For example, Webmaster could have worked with WQW to amend their patents by adding members of the Webmaster team as coinventors. If Webmaster was not interested in a joint agreement, it could have filed its own patents first *or* gone to court to litigate for all or partial ownership of the patent disclosure.

Poor understanding of cultural and philosophical differences.
WQW assumed that Webmaster would continue to see the project through at its initial resource level. Their reasoning was that full staffing is needed to ensure timeliness and quality. Webmaster, on the other hand, did not want to lose momentum in other projects and was more concerned with the big picture. Its management did the logical thing for the business: transfer key people to a new project as the old one winds down—the time-phased staffing described in Chapter 3.

As I described in Chapter 2, this clash is the result of philosophical differences. In the US, effective management policy tends to emphasize minimum expenses and maximum profits, which in turn dictates moving people off a project before, or shortly after, a project is completed. The Japanese, on the other hand, keep their teams together longer to ensure that the product meets the customer expectations and is sufficiently high quality.

The philosophical difference was compounded by the gap in the two companies' investments. WQW invested much more, so it felt it had more at stake if the project failed. By the way, this may be true in absolute dollar terms, but not necessarily in relative terms. That is, the investment could be a percentage of revenue or sales for each company.

Conglomerate Inc.

Conglomerate Inc. is an international Fortune 500 company with operating units and divisions in every continent. Its sales are over $40 billion and it has a highly decentralized management structure. Their two major market segments and revenue sources are government contracting and commercial product development.

The Arrangement

Conglomerate's corporate planners had decided that one of its electronics divisions should emphasize the home security market in Europe and the US. According to a market survey documented in a business case and some initial conceptual research and development activities, an ultrasonic home intrusion system was deemed the ideal product to pursue. Because requirements and marketing were different between Europe and the US, management decided to have the North American and European design centers jointly develop a core set of design building blocks. In this way, they hoped to cover a reasonably broad base of fundamental requirements. Conglomerate would then tailor the configuration of the building blocks for individual market segments.

The Project

Management chose design centers in Ft. Wayne, Indiana and Frankfurt, Germany to form the virtual team. There were 70 members in Ft. Wayne and 77 members in Frankfurt. The Ft. Wayne developers were grouped under a program manager in a very loose organization, with decision making at the lowest level. The Frankfurt developers were structured in a very hierarchical organization, with decisions having to make their way up the organizational ladder. To facilitate joint software and product development, the team at Ft. Wayne duplicated the intranet at the Frankfurt design center as a back-up facility.

Program updates were circulated weekly. The team conducted other communications via e-mail, telephone, and video conferences. All documents were electronic so that they could be easily stored and retrieved.

The first task was to develop requirements for the products. The Ft. Wayne group was able to finalize its set of requirements tasks relatively quickly, but because the Frankfurt group had several levels of management reviews, changes, and approvals, activities got bogged down. This delayed both teams' entry into the design phase.

The Difficulties

As design progressed, the team decided to partition the system into subsystems to minimize the overlap of responsibility. Despite this strategy, there seemed to be continual second-guessing on design decisions between the two centers. Even though the team agreed to develop the operating system design in Ft. Wayne and have the design reviewed in Frankfurt, the Frankfurt team began developing its own operating system in secret. Unfortunately, the program manager failed to travel to Frankfurt often enough to build relationships and verify design details. He was not given complete information and did not check into details until it was too late.

The Frankfurt designers completed their application software ahead of schedule, but it operated only on their operating system design, not on the design being done in Ft. Wayne. Tension between the two design centers began to rise. It didn't help that the marketing department, eager to show something to customers, took the Frankfurt design and started marketing it worldwide.

The project continued with difficulty. Communications remained cordial, but schedules slipped. The Ft. Wayne design center continued to document all the software design, test, and requirements; the Frankfurt design center didn't feel that was necessary. The project was late but still relatively close to its target completion date.

As the product launch drew near, many engineers in the Ft. Wayne center sacrificed their summer vacations. Meanwhile, the Frankfurt design center shut down for several weeks, as the team observed the summer holiday. The Ft. Wayne team was surprised and dismayed that the Frankfurt team had not made a similar sacrifice. The project was delayed another month until the Frankfurt designers got back from their vacation.

After the product was developed and shipped directly to retailers, customers began to report performance problems. The Frankfurt designers did not want to consider the possibility of problems with their software unless there was proof that the faulty performance was in something they had responsibility for. The Frankfurt team solved interface problems between software packages by rewriting the software completed in Ft. Wayne to accommodate their designs. Things degenerated from there, and in the end, Conglomerate had the design centers take their separate designs and build separate but functionally equivalent products.

Analysis

There are several points in this case study:

Poor understanding of responsibility and accountability. Getting two engineering centers thousands of miles apart to agree on an approach is difficult enough in the same country and culture. Conglomerate management falsely assumed that, because the two divisions had similar skills and market interests, they would naturally be driven to work closely together. They neglected to explore project expectations and possible problems early in the project. Because the teams were not prepped on cultural differences and differences in organizational structure, they rapidly became frustrated with each other's methods.

As I describe in Chapter 5, cultural differences often cause divergent decision making. The Ft. Wayne team had a structure that let it make decisions more quickly and move the project along. In a traditional German organization, hierarchy rules the decisions most US organizations make at the lowest level. The expectations of the two centers were founded on a poor understanding of what to expect from each other, and neither center adjusted its decision making to reach some middle ground that both could live with. This led to frustration and conflict.

Weak central leadership. When the team differs in its cultural and organizational expectations, it is up to the leaders to assert a workable compromise. If this leadership is lacking, as it obviously was in this case, local leadership will fulfill its self interests. The disagreements on the approach of the operating system and the lack of strong project leadership set the Frankfurt team up to ignore the design responsibilities of the Ft. Wayne team.

As I said earlier, the program manager should have made the teams' respective expectations clear to everyone early in the project. For example, explaining that European countries tend to shut down operations for several weeks at various times, including late summer, would have adjusted the Ft. Wayne team's expectations and allowed them the choice of taking a summer vacation.

The program manager should have also met with the Frankfurt team frequently face to face.

Lack of trust and confusion about ownership. When creating a virtual organization, project managers must be alert for extreme differences in technical directions. In this case, the program manager could have spent more time and money establishing personal relationships with the two local leaders early in the project. He could have also had members from each team work with the other team for three or four months. Finally, as the project progressed, he should have taken an emotional pulse and instituted corrective actions such as weekly meetings to address schedule milestones and each team's critical issues. These actions would have established an atmosphere of cooperative problem-solving. It's a common mistake to think you can build trust by technology alone; as I describe in Chapter 6, there is no substitute for face-to-face in building personal relationships.

Candoit Inc.

Candoit has its roots in supplying software contract personnel to various companies. Over the last several years, it started to expand its services by bidding and winning small software development and testing contracts to local companies. One of the company's strategic missions was to double its sales revenue in three years—a planned, managed growth to make Candoit a more significant player in the contract and software services market. To meet this goal, the sales managers had started to bid more aggressively on larger projects with more potential for revenue.

There was a major celebration when Candoit won its first million-dollar-plus software development contract to deliver several test stations that run on standard PCs networked together. The terms and conditions negotiated included a fixed-price contract with initial monies paid at the beginning of the project and payments tied to various development milestones. The price they bid to win the job was very close to the estimates they had prepared, but top management felt that greater efficiencies could be realized, which they would determine later. The completed product was due to the customer in 18 months.

The Arrangement

The project began as a nonvirtual project, with Candoit doing all the work. Four months into the project, there were signs of trouble. Staffing up to the expected level was delayed by several months, causing slips in the initial design reviews with the customer. Six months into the project, Candoit realized it had underestimated requirements for both staff and cost. The project was two months behind schedule and top management was looking for a solution. They bought expensive CASE tools and the project team worked longer hours, but the needed efficiencies were not being achieved. Candoit began channeling personnel from other projects to help out, delaying potential revenues from those projects. Eight months into the project the forecast was break-even profit at best.

A little desperate at this point, Candoit decided to outsource the network administration part of the software, since that was its weakest area of expertise and represented a large area of potential cost savings. The company accepted a very low bid from Network Solutions, a small software company in India. Although they felt this approach might be risky, the financial picture looked attractive and it would put profits back to the earlier projection.

The Project

Candoit hastily generated a statement of work and negotiated a fixed-price cost structure that would have Network Solutions deliver the network administration software in six months. Network Solutions was to receive half the money right away and the remainder when the software was delivered. As part of the contract, Network Solutions was to use the development tools Candoit specified.

The project team consisted of 12 members from Candoit and six members from Network Solutions. The vice president of custom applications coordinated the outsourcing, and English was the project language.

Interfacing with Network Solutions took more effort than anticipated. The Candoit project team was up late many nights on conference calls after working long days on other problems. There were volumes of e-mail and faxes.

The Difficulties

Five months into the subcontract, Candoit received an integration build from Network Solutions. When the Candoit team integrated it, the software didn't meet Candoit's functionality. The Candoit team was puzzled. They had spent a lot of time communicating how functions should be implemented, yet many functions had not been implemented according to their instructions. Even though the tools were compatible, the software was different enough in subtle ways to make it seem as if a different compiler version had been used.

Network Solutions estimated that it would take three more months to fix these problems, and it wanted the remaining money before making the changes and additional money after completion. Candoit had no choice but to agree to these requests, having put itself in a vulnerable position.

When Candoit received the final code from Network Solutions, there were still problems, but Network Solutions had decided that it had met the terms and conditions of the contract and declined to work on any additional changes. To preserve the schedule, Candoit had to change the Network Solutions software so that it could deliver the integrated software package to the customer. The project was delivered four months late and Candoit ended up with a financial loss.

Analysis

Candoit made many mistakes, probably because it did not think through the outsourcing but was forced into it by underestimating the project work and cost in the first place. In fact, that was actually its first mistake.

Outsourcing under pressure.   Using outsourcing to solve cost and schedule problems rarely works. As I describe in Chapter 3, outsourcing should be planned, not a last resort to wipe away pressing problems. The way Candoit outsourced its work to Network Solutions provided no time to build a business relationship. Consequently, Network Solutions felt no ownership of the software it produced, which manifested in an unwillingness to be flexible for Candoit and a strong focus on cost issues.

Poor choice of cost structure.   Candoit chose the wrong cost structure for this project. As I describe in Chapter 3, the fixed-price cost structure usually ends up with the contractor losing money when it is applied to a project with an expected slim profit margin. This structure works more effectively on products with long run rates, where efficiencies can be gained in the manufacturing process and purchasing cost-downs placed on suppliers. Software products do not fit this type of model due to the inherent risks associated with intellectual endeavors.

Throwing more resources at a troubled project.   Candoit thought that by using the latest CASE tools and extended overtime it could make large gains in efficiency. This strategy rarely works because tools rarely meet all the expectations their vendors have set, and management tends to underestimate the learning curve. People, not tools, must solve complex problems. With new tools, people end up solving new-tool problems, instead of software development problems.

Poorly defined statement of work.   Candoit's expectations for the project didn't seem to find their way into the statement of work. Instead, Candoit threw the statement together just so that software development could begin. As I describe in Chapter 3, any statement of work should detail expectations and include a functional requirements specification and a development plan to address detailed project milestones, configuration control, the use of tools, and so on. If the statement of work does not spell out these elements, it should refer to documents that do. It should also address quality and warranty expectations after delivery.

Unclear explanation of tool use. Candoit and Network Solutions agreed to use similar tools, but they neglected to agree on the details about the tool versions. This may seem like a small point, but small points like this can cause larger issues during software integration, as it did in this case. Each company should be responsible for its own tool problems unless they specify otherwise early on. By making all the details of tool use clear to all parties, companies can avoid software problems such as fixing new tool problems or revisiting problems that have already been fixed.

11
Epilogue: The Virtual Future

As this book has pointed out, there are already many challenges in performing software development in an international setting. In the future, things will only be more difficult. Technological advances will continue to make the world smaller and more companies will experience scenarios even more complex than those presented here.

Virtual software projects will soon be nearly inevitable. Market pressure and evolving technology will combine to demand more intricate projects and a more flexible project structure to handle the diverse organizational patterns that must mesh to produce a satisfactory product. There are increasingly fewer opportunities to rely strictly on internal resources for software development. Evolving computer and software technology will continue to encourage cottage industries of specialized individuals and small groups. This will lead to more partnerships and subcontracting, since most companies cannot technically or financially keep up with all the types of technical innovation. As a result, companies will concentrate on core software technologies that are most closely related to their products. Other industries, such as the automotive and aeronautics, have already experienced this shift. Products became more complex as the technology outpaced the manufacturers' ability to use their internal resources.

Software development is now better managed, and there are signs that it is also headed down the global development path. An example is application-specific integrated circuits. The ASIC community had believed the ASICs had to be developed and fabricated locally. But today an ASIC can be designed in one facility, fabricated in another, packaged in a third, and tested in a fourth—with all the facilities geographically distant from each other. ASIC manufacturers were driven to lower costs. The same pressure will drive global software development as well.

Global software centers outside the US are appearing in India, Israel, and the Pacific Rim, but software developers will not be able to realize the same success that ASIC manufacturers have enjoyed unless they put a management structure in place to handle virtual development and produce high-quality software.

With software being developed at different locations and with schedule pressures increasing, companies will begin to look to software architectures. Architectures will be expected to be more elastic to handle different software structures, be easily changeable, and be more tolerant to errors. Software architecture will be the focal point to handle integration issues between software and hardware subsystems and the user, requiring architecture to be more robust than in the past. Moreover, the codevelopment problems we now see between software and hardware platform development will change. The current emphasis to adapt the software to the hardware's limitations and parameters will shift to designing a more flexible hardware platform to accommodate software changes. The reason is that most of the product value will be in the software, not the hardware.

Organization structure and business practices will adapt to the changing landscape of how products are developed and marketed. More subcontracts and other types of business relationships will be used to contribute to virtual projects along with identifying individuals who can work away from the office environment.

The software marketplace will continue to grow and designs will continue to become less specific to any one country or culture. The use of icons in many operating systems and in products such as Microsoft's Windows can be found in almost all countries. The Internet will continue to push business into on-line virtual products and services. The people and businesses that are comfortable with the technology will be the leaders. Likewise, the Internet will continue to promote more common standards for user interfaces, which will make software development easier to develop for the international market because there will be fewer features that are unique to a country's native language and culture.

But no matter where the future leads, the past has proved that management—not technology—will make companies successful in the software market. Managers are trained to be decision makers, and they make the best decisions when they are informed. The information I have presented here has hopefully contributed to more educated decision making and thus has better prepared managers to handle an increasingly global work environment.

A

Tutorial on Intellectual Property Protection

When dealing with software development in a competitive market, you want your product to have some features that set it apart from other products. You may identify unique features through market surveys, research and development activities, or during design. To maintain and protect your product's uniqueness, you need to use one of several methods for protecting intellectual property. This appendix is only to acquaint you with the basics of the methods and the patent process [1] used in the US and overseas. You should consult an attorney before deciding which method is most suitable for your specific situation.

Trade Secrets

A trade secret is a formula, device, or information with three properties:

- It is not generally publicly known or readily available.

- It is kept secret by those who do know it.

- It is used in business to provide an advantage over competitors who do not know or use it.

A trade secret can also be proprietary information or technology—including software—that is not accessible to the market. In this case, the information or technology must

- provide some commercial advantage from being kept secret,

- not be accessible from publicly available information or generally known, and

129

- be subject to reasonable measures to maintain secrecy.

Trade secrets enjoy a limited degree of legal protection under state laws; the scope of protection varies from state to state. Generally the holder of a trade secret has a right to expect that competitors will not use improper means to discover it. The trade secret holder has no right to prevent a competitor from using the trade secret if the competitor discovered the trade secret legitimately.

Because the effectiveness of trade secret protection depends on secrecy, it is understandably difficult to use trade secret laws as a basis for protecting mass-marketed software. The more users who have access to the software, the less likely the software's details can be kept hidden from the competition. Some software publishers have attempted to impose secrecy obligations on their users by attaching restrictive agreements to the outside of the software package—the so-called "shrink wrap" agreements.

Trade secret protection can be very useful for software that is intended for a small market, including engineering software, software used in manufacturing plants, and certain software used in financial markets. It is not uncommon for the software owner to insist that each user sign a use agreement that severely restricts the users' right to disclose the software to others. Through such restrictive agreements, the secrecy, and thus the trade secret status of the software, is preserved.

Copyrights

Copyrights are the legal tool most commonly relied on to protect software. A copyright is a form of legal protection established by federal law (Title 17 of the US Code). Copyrights are quite literally the exclusive legal right to copy an original work of authorship and to prevent others from copying the work. Common works of authorship include written texts (such as this book), songs, sculpture, and audiovisual works (movies or video games, or the artistic screens of a piece of commercial software). Most software products are considered original works of authorship.

Copyrights, although popular, have two important limitations.

- *They protect only the artistic expression of ideas or concepts, not the ideas or concepts, themselves.* For example, if a paper were to describe a novel invention, the copyright on the paper would not prevent someone from using the described invention, nor would it prevent someone from publishing a different description of the invention. It would only prevent another person from copying the particular description in the paper.

- *They prohibit only the copying of the protected work.* If another author were to independently develop a work identical in all respects to an earlier, copyrighted work, the individual would not be violating the earlier copyright by publishing his work. On the other hand, loading a piece of software from a CD ROM into a computer memory does constitute "copying" the software, as does keying in a piece of code from a printed listing.

No special steps are necessary to create a copyright, which is one reason they are so popular. Patents, for example, are much harder to obtain. A person who writes a piece of software automatically has copyright protection on the work, according to copyright law. However, copyrights must be registered in the US Library of Congress before you can sue anyone for violating your copyright.

Trademarks

A trademark is any mark applied to a product to distinguish it from competing products. After a period, customers come to identify the trademark with the company using the mark and with their experiences (good and bad) with the products. Hence, the trademark carries the company's goodwill and reputation. Under state laws (common law and statutory law) and federal laws (Title 15, Chapter 22 of the US Code) it is improper for someone to use another person's trademark on his own products without the permission of the trademark owner. A trademark prevents other companies from profiting through trading on the reputation of a competitor. It also protects the company's investments in marketing, advertising, and so on, from which they have built their reputation and customer goodwill.

The mark itself may be anything that distinguishes the products or services of one company from another. Examples are words, symbols, icons, packaging, design, shape, sound and even smell.

To establish trademark rights, you merely need to use the mark with your products or services. You can also file an application for trademark registration with the US Patent and Trademark Office, which indicates that you intend to use a trademark. Trademark rights continue as long as the owner continues to use the trademark on his products. With such continued use, the trademark may endure forever.

A trademark does not prevent others from copying the technology embodied in the trademarked product. Thus for most software products, trademarks provides very little protection for the unique features that make a product competitive.

Mask Works

Mask work protection is available for semiconductor mask works as a result of the Semiconductor Chip Protection Act (in Title 17, Chapter 9 of the US Code). This type of protection is useful for software embedded in hardware. The SCPA grants the owner of a mask work the exclusive right to reproduce the mask work and to distribute chips containing the mask work. The SCPA does not prohibit others from reverse-engineering the mask to understand the idea, process, system, method of operation, concept, or principle embodied in the mask work.

For software embedded in silicon, mask works do not protect the concepts and ideas embodied in the software.

Patents

Patents protect inventions embodied in products and processes. Under US patent law (Title 35 of the US Code), the patent holder has the exclusive right to make, use, and sell the patented invention. Someone who makes, uses, or sells a product incorporating the patented invention without the permission of the patent owner infringes on the patent. The life of a US patent is 20 years from the date the patent application was filed. When the patent expires, the invention becomes part of the public domain; anyone can then use the invention.

A patented invention, unlike a trade secret, must be disclosed to the public. Patent law requires that an inventor describe the invention in enough detail that someone skilled in the art can understand and use it. Because the description becomes part of the patent, competitors will know the details of the invention as soon as the patent issues. However, they are not permitted to use the patented features for the life of the patent.

Patents are not easy to obtain. For an idea to be patented, it must be novel and objectively unobvious, from the perspective of the typical person practicing in the relevant area of technology. There is some subjectivity involved in determining what is "novel or unobviousness," and many inventors frequently have a rather different opinion on the subject than the US Patent and Trademark Office during the initial phases of their patent application reviews. For example, in one patent application, which is still under review, the inventor used a modified communication protocol in a new application. The dispute between the patent examiner and inventor centered around the novel aspects of using a technology in an application it wasn't designed for.

Concepts and ideas embodied in software are patentable. Patents are relatively expensive and a significant investment of effort and time is necessary to prepare and file a patent application. After the application is filed in the US Patent and Trademark Office, you then must wait about two years for a patent to issue. However, the strong advantages of patents outweigh the cost and wait in many cases.

Advantages of Patenting

A patent prevents others from using the patented invention, even if they came up with the product independently. Thus, patents protect the investment made in the development of the invention and in bringing it to market. Likewise, if the product is copied and market share erodes, patents provide a legal framework to pursue lost profits.

Another advantage is that patents may cause other companies to abandon or modify their product development activities once they learn that certain technologies or processes are covered by a patent. This may lead competitors to extend their product's time to market so as to avoid encroaching on your patent and consequently may give you leverage in negotiating with your customers.

Finally, a patent holder can obtain revenue by granting royalty-bearing licenses to other companies or by selling the patent.

What Can Be Patented?

Patents are especially appropriate when you are developing a new technology. The patentability of software has been a somewhat contentious issue under the law. Software itself is rather intangible and operates in many cases on an unobvious level. It is perhaps not surprising that some software inventions initially met with resistance in the US Patent and Trademark Office because of its position that "methods of doing business and laws of nature are not patentable." Since the first software patent in 1968, the interpretation of what can be patented as software has changed.

At one end of the spectrum, it is clear that you cannot obtain a patent on a mathematical formula or algorithm per se. If a patent were permitted to cover an equation, the patent would preempt all uses of the mathematical expression, such as in a sort routine, net present value of money, and so on. At the opposite extreme, a machine or other device using software (for example, a test station that uses software to sample voltages and currents to determine if the product works) would be considered patentable. A gray area exists at some point between these two extremes, but for the most part, software inventions that are tied to real world problems and systems are now considered to be legitimate candidates for patent protection. Most software patents today relate to embedded applications, computer implemented business aids, or user/computer interfaces.

The patent process that involves software usually takes longer than most other types of patents categories, generally more than two years on the average from filing to the issue of the patent. By US law, the right to obtain a patent on an invention is lost if the patent application is not filed within one year after the invention was first put in public use or on sale, or the invention was first described in a printed publication. Talk to a patent attorney if you have questions about this important loss of right issue. The following describes the patent filing process at the US Patent and Trademark Office.

The Patenting Process

The patenting process has many steps, but if you have the resources, they need not be complicated.

Search for Prior Art

The first step is to search for prior inventions (also known as prior art) that are similar to the technology or product you want to develop. The US Patent and Trademark Office has developed the US Patent and Classification System, which lets users store and retrieve patents according to subject matter. Patents are organized into classes and subclasses of subject areas in the US Patent and Trademark Office's *Manual of Classification* [2]. The *US Patent Classification System* [3] contains an index into various classes and subclasses.

To search for patents issued after 1970, you can use the US Patent and Trademark Office's Automated Patent System. The system lets you search according to the classes, subclasses, and terms used in the patent classification. You can access Automated Patent System terminals in the US Patent and Trademark Office building in Arlington, Virginia, and at some of the Patent and Trademark Depository Libraries (universities, municipal, state, and special research institutions that receive and maintain collections of patents and trademarks for public use). For a list of depository libraries, contact the US Patent and Trademark Office (www.uspto.gov). You can also search for patents via the Web, as I describe later.

The resources of the US Patent and Trade Office are not the only ones available for patent searches. Commercial databases and CD ROMs include

- *IFI/Plenum Data Company's CLAIMS*. Covers US patents and includes front-page information on the patent, such as a descriptive abstract and a diagram of the invention.

- *WPI*. Global but provides limited information about patents issued in many countries around the world. Provides the patent title and abstract.

- *INPADOC.* Also global but with limited information about foreign patents. Provides patent family coverage, including bibliographic data, patent family, and legal status.

Although the up-front cost of using CD ROMs and associated search software is significant, there is no additional cost. On-line databases are also a good choice because you can get continual updates without buying another software package.

The Web provides a wealth of resources—some commercial, some free—devoted to patents and patent searching. At the time of this writing, IBM was maintaining a Web site (http://patent.womplex.ibm.com) that let users search all US patents issued since 1971 at no cost. The Web site provides access to patent drawings for most of the patents.

Application and Examination

If your search reveals no prior art, the next step is to submit a patent application to the US Patent and Trademark Office. Figure A.1 summarizes the major steps in the patent process from submission to patent approval.

A patent application describes and illustrates the invention. It follows a prescribed format and concludes with one or more patent claims. A patent claim is the written definition of the invention for which you are seeking to cover. Once you complete the patent application, you submit it to the US Patent and Trademark Office via express courier. Electronic submission is not allowed.

When the US Patent and Trademark Office receives the application, it notifies you of receipt, classifies the application according to the type of technology, and assigns it to a patent examiner who has expertise in the subject. The examiner then searches for prior art to determine if the invention is new and unobvious. The search covers current US patents, foreign patents, professional journals, and other related sources of documentation. The examiner's review of the application explores such issues as

- *Is the disclosure adequate?* Does it cover all the information required for a patent application. Is the filing fee attached?

- *Does it comply with formal and legal requirements?* Is the application in the proper format, for example?

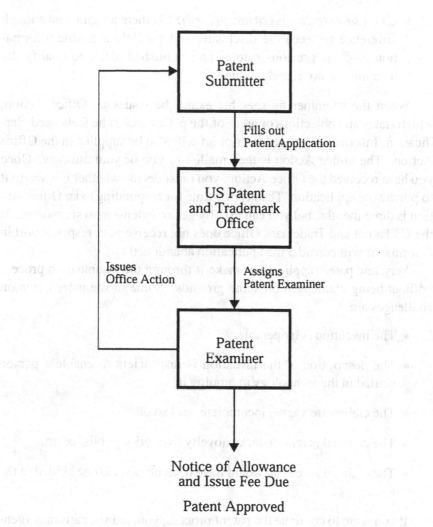

Notice of Allowance
and Issue Fee Due

Patent Approved

Figure A.1: Summary of the major steps in the US patent process.

- *Is the invention operable?* Will it work and can it be used commercially?

- *Can it be patented, given any prior art?* Is there a significant enough difference between the disclosure and publicly available information, such as previous patents and published ideas, to qualify the invention as novel and unique?

When the examiner finishes his exam, he issues an Office Action, which states any objections or areas of the patent claims he feels need clarification. Information related to prior art will also be supplied in the Office Action. The Office Action is then mailed to you or your attorney. Once you have received the Office Action, you must decide whether it is worth it to pursue the application. The normal time for responding to an Office Action is three months, but you can usually get an extension to six months. If the US Patent and Trademark Office does not receive your response within that time, it will consider the application abandoned.

Very few patent applications make it through the examination process without being challenged on some grounds. Some of the more common challenges are

- The invention is inoperable.

- The description of the invention is insufficient to enable a person skilled in the technology to employ it.

- The claims are vague, incomplete, and so on.

- The claimed invention lacks novelty over prior published art.

- The claimed invention would have been obvious to one skilled in the art.

If you want to continue the patent process, you and your attorney (generally you will act through an attorney at this point) need to prepare a written response to the Office Action to explain or clarify issues related to each rejected claim. You can also change the wording of the patent claims to improve or alter the description of the claimed invention. The patent examiner then reviews the patent application in light of your comments and changes and either approves the patent with modified wording or issues a second Office Action. The second Office Action is final unless you appeal it, but you can refile the application if you want to change the patent claims again. If the claims in the patent are accepted, the examiner sends a Notice of Allowance and Issue Fee Due and your patent is typically issued about three months after the office receives the issues fee. The fee can be anywhere from $490 to $980, depending on the length of the application and the number of claims made.

Patent Rights in US Government Software Contracts

When you are developing software for the US government, the request for proposal and contract usually reference the parts of the Federal Acquisition Regulations (FAR) and/or the Defense Federal Acquisition Regulations Supplement (DFARS) that relate to ownership of rights to intellectual property, which includes rights to software. Under FAR and DFARS, the government generally receives unlimited rights to software developed under government contracts. This includes software that is

- the result of a government contract,

- required to be developed under the government contract or generated as a part of the contract,

- a database, developed under government contract, which includes information supplied by the government, information in which the government has unlimited rights, or is public domain,

- software provided by the government and modified,

- publicly available or released by a contractor without restrictions.

"Unlimited rights" in this context means that the government can copy the software and give it to other government agencies or contractors for use on government contracts without paying you anything additional.

If you developed the software at your own expense before the contract, you can petition for the government to have only restricted rights to the software. However,

- The contract specifying restricted rights must incorporate an agreement that the software is being provided only with restricted rights.

- There must be a license agreement to identify the rights to be given to the government.

- The software must be marked with the proper legend.

- The software documentation must refer to the software rights limitations.

Restricted rights means the government may use the software only on the computer for which it was acquired or on a backup machine if the original computer is inoperative. The government may also copy the software only for archiving or backing up and may use the software with other software only if the end product is subject to the same restrictive rights as the original software.

Foreign Patents

US patents are effective only in the US. If you need patent protection in other countries, you must file patent applications in those countries. Obtaining patents in foreign countries is relatively complicated because each country has its own set of patent laws and because various regional and international treaties exist that specify special processes and rules for the international filing of patent applications.

There are three general methods through which you can seek patents outside the US.

Apply for a patent for each individual country. This typically requires translating the patent application into the country's national language—a process that may take several months, since many technical terms may not have direct translations and other terms may have to be substituted. Once you submit the application, you are almost always challenged by some country's patent examiner because the patent process and examiners vary widely from country to country.

Use the European Patent Convention to obtain a European patent. This method works only if you are filing an application in multiple European countries. The EPC covers Austria, Belgium, Denmark, France, Great Britain, Greece, Germany, Ireland, Italy, Luxembourg, Monaco, The Netherlands, Portugal, Spain, Sweden, and Switzerland. You send the EPC patent application to the European Patent Office (EPO) headquarters in Munich, Germany. For each country, the EPO charges a designation fee plus a one-time application fee. Most patents issued in Europe have 10 or fewer claims to help reduce filing costs. Additional charges are assessed for excess claims.

The EPC patent application can be completed in English, and processed and examined in English, which saves money and makes it easier to supervise the process. Once the EPO has issued the patent, you must still register the European patent individually in each designated country. Most European countries require that translations be filed at that time. The advantage of EPC patent application is that there is no further need to examine the merits of the invention.

File an international application using the Patent Cooperation Treaty. Approximately 55 countries have signed the PCT, including those in the EPC. The PCT application is a relatively recent innovation, but it does not replace any of the other processes. No PCT patent is granted; instead, after the examination is complete, the PCT patent application is forwarded to the individual countries or to the EPC, depending on the countries selected. Compared to the other foreign filing methods, the PCT patent application adds cost, complexity, and time to patent filing. However, you can file a PCT patent application very quickly and relatively inexpensively. You can also delay many of your foreign filing costs for about a year. As with any patent filing, you should use an attorney trained in the patent process to avoid costly mistakes and delays, especially when filing foreign patents.

No matter which method you choose, you must not have disclosed the invention to the public prior to filing a patent application in the US, and you must not file the foreign application later than one year from the US patent filing date. There are few exceptions to these rules.

Bibliography

[1] M. Lechter, *Successful Patents and Patenting for Engineers and Scientists*, IEEE Press, New York, 1995.

[2] *Manual of Classification*, US Government Printing Office, Mail List Section, Washington, DC, 20402.

[3] *US Patent Classification System*, US Government Printing Office, Mail List Section, Washington, DC, 20402.

B

What Happens When?

This appendix is a tool for planning the virtual project. The milestone chart below shows the activities described in this book in an at-a-glance format. Below are some brief descriptions of the activity with pointers to chapters that offer more detail.

- *Finalize business arrangement.* Identify and agree on the type and structure of the business arrangement used in developing the software, such as joint venture or strategic partnership.—Chapter 1

- *Identify virtual team.* Identify the structure, members, and member roles, and responsibilities of the software team.—Chapters 2, 5

- *Identify virtual technology.* Identify the technical infrastructure that team members will use to communicate with each other (video conferencing, e-mail, groupware, and so on).—Chapters 2, 6

- *Define statement of work.* Create the document used to identify the software development responsibilities and expectations between the customer (organization requesting outsourcing, for example) and supplier.—Chapter 3

- *Divide the work.* Divide the effort among software developers by staffing, business relationship, expertise level, and so on.—Chapter 4

- *Identify tools and methods.* Identify the software development tools and design and development methods, such as testing simulators or Joint Application Development, that the virtual team will use.—Chapters 5, 8

- *Establish virtual SCCB.* Identify the members of the Software Configuration Control Board, the method they will use for software configuration management, and how frequently they will meet.—Chapters 5, 7

- *Identify and manage risks.* Identify risks and devise a risk mitigation strategy for each class of risk. As the milestone chart shows, this activity should go on during every phase of the development life cycle.—Chapters 2, 7

- *Control documentation.* Identify a control method, such as project folders indexed by subject or author, and apply it to all project documentation.—Chapter 7.

- *Develop and apply test suites.* Identify test suites during software design and code development. During testing, perform software verification and validation using test suites.—Chapter 8

- *Develop and apply traceability matrix.* Create the matrix during requirements and update it during design and code generation. The matrix traces software tests to requirements, code to design, and design to requirements.—Chapter 8

- *Develop and apply module version matrix.* This matrix identifies a piece of code (module) to the configuration version it uses in a software build.—Chapter 8

- *Establish maintenance review board.* This board reviews requests for changes after the product has been delivered to the customer.—Chapter 9

- *Control software quality.* Perform activities that enhance the software's quality and ensure that the software meets the customer's expectations. Activities include design reviews, code inspections, and testing.—Chapter 5

- *Manage intellectual property.* Perform activities, such as design reviews, to determine if ideas generated during development should be protected as intellectual property.—Appendix A

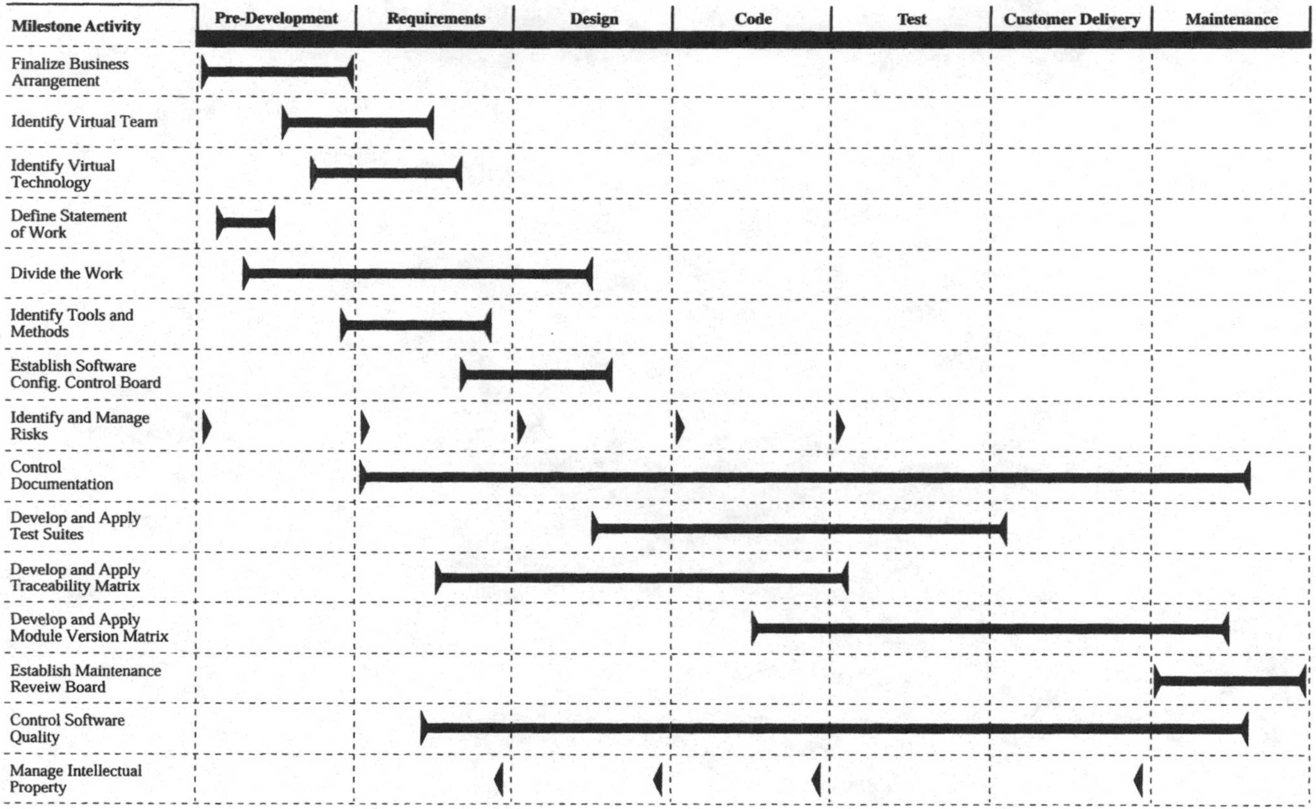

Figure B.1: Major milestones for virtual projects.

C

Major International Software Quality Standards

The following are standards segregated by country or region. The standards immediately below are considered global.

Global Standards

- International Atomic Energy Agency (IAEA), TRS-282, *Manual on Quality Assurance for Computer Software Related to the Safety of Nuclear Power Plants*—www.iaca.or.at/worldatom/

- International Organization for Standardization (ISO), *ISO 9000-3, Quality Management and Quality Assurance Standards—Part 3: Guidelines for the Application of ISO 9001 to the Development, Supply, and Maintenance of Software*—www.iso.ch/9000e/9k14ke.htm

European Standards

- British Standards Institute (BSI), *BSI BS 7165, Recommendations for Achievement of Quality in Software*—www.open.gov.uk

- *British Defence Standard (DEF) DEF 00-16/ISS1, Guide to Achievement of Quality in Software*—www.dstan.mod.uk

- United Kingdom Department of Trade and Industry (DTI), *DTI TickIT, Guide to Software Quality Management Systems Construction and Certification*—www.dti.gov.uk

- European Space Agency (ESA), *ESA PSS-05-11, Guide to Software Quality Assurance*—dxsting.cern.ch/sting/ESA.txt

- Federation of the Electronics Industry (FEI), *Establishing a Quality Assurance Function for Software*—fm6.facility.pipex.com/fei

- Institution of Electrical Engineers (IEE), *IEE6, Software Quality Assurance: Model Procedures*—www.iee.org.uk/inspea.html

- North Atlantic Treaty Organization (NATO), *NATO AQAP-150, Quality Assurance Requirements for Software Development*—www.vm.ee/nato/docu/stanag/aqap150/aqap150e.html

North American Standards

- Canadian Standards Association (CSA), *CSA CAN/CSA-396, Guide for Selecting and Implementing the CAN/CSA Q396-89 Software Quality Assurance Program Standards*—www.ihs.on.ca/engineering/standard/csa.htm

- Canadian Standards Association (CSA), *CSA CAN/CSA-396.11, Quality Assurance Program for Development of Software Used in Critical Applications*—www.ihs.on.ca/engineering/standard/csa.htm

- US Department of Defense (DoD), *Mil-Std-1535B, Supplier Quality Assurance Program Requirements*—www.dsmc.dsm.mil/pubs/pmnotebook/pmn7-2.htm

- US Federal Aviation Authority (FAA), *FAA STD-018a, Computer Software Quality Program Requirements*—www.nasi.hq.faa.gov/nasiHTML/FAAStandards/index .html

- US Federal Food and Drug Administration (FDA), *FDA 90-4236, Pre-production Quality Assurance Planning: Recommendations for Medical Device Manufacturers*—www.fda.gov/search.html

- Institute of Electrical and Electronics Engineers (IEEE), *IEEE 730, Software Quality Plans, IEEE 730.1, Guide for Software Assurance Planning, IEEE 1061, Software Quality Assurance: Documentation Reviews*—standards.ieee.org

- Nuclear Regulatory Commission (NRC), *NRC NUREG/BR-0167, Software Quality Assurance Programs and Guidelines*—www.nrc.edu/gov/NRC/index.html

Pacific Rim Standards

Australia: *AS 3563.1, Software Quality Management System: Part 1, Requirements, AS 3563.2, Software Quality Management System: Part 2, Implementation Guide, AS/NZS 3905.8, Quality System Guidelines*—www.dpc.vic.gov.au/ocmpol/218e.htm

Pacific Rim Standards

List of Figures

List of Tables

About the Author

Dr. Dale Walter Karolak is an engineering director at TRW Automotive Electronics, where he is responsible for product development for domestic and international customers. His previous positions include software and systems engineering manager at ITT Aerospace/Communications, and software engineer at GTE Communications Systems R&D Laboratories. He is the creator of the Just-in-Time software development methodology, holds a patent on the Communications Management System Architecture, and has three patents pending in software architecture and communication.

Dr. Karolak has headed virtual software development ventures worldwide, including the US, Europe, and the Middle East. His projects typically involve domestic and international companies and project teams of from 10 to 70 members. At present, he is assessing a joint US-European project to produce an automotive safety-critical product, and is currently conducting a series of joint design reviews.

Dr. Karolak received a PhD in software engineering from Union Institute, an MBA from the University of Phoenix, and a BS in computer science from Central Michigan University. He is the author of the IEEE Computer Society's bestseller *Software Engineering Risk Management* and developer of SERIM, the product that evolved from the book. Dr. Karolak is a frequent speaker at international conferences and has published widely in software management, metrics, reliability, quality, testing, and architecture. He is a member of the IEEE, IEEE Computer Society, ACM, and Society of Automotive Engineers.

Dr. Karolak can be contacted at dkarolak@ieee.org.

Index

Press Activities Board

IEEE Computer Society Publications

The world-renowned IEEE Computer Society publishes, promotes, and distributes a wide variety of authoritative computer science and engineering texts. These books are available from most retail outlets. The IEEE Computer Society is seeking new practitioner-oriented and leading-edge research titles in computer science and computer engineering. Visit the Online Catalog, http://computer.org, for a list of products and new author information.

Submission of proposals: For guidelines and information on the IEEE Computer Society books, send e-mail to cs.books@computer.org or write to the Project Editor, IEEE Computer Society, P.O. Box 3014, 10662 Los Vaqueros Circle, Los Alamitos, CA 90720-1314. Telephone +1 714-821-8380. FAX +1 714-761-1784.

IEEE Computer Society Proceedings

The IEEE Computer Society also produces and actively promotes the proceedings of more than 130 acclaimed international conferences each year in multimedia formats that include hard and softcover books, CD-ROMs, videos, and on-line publications.

For information on the IEEE Computer Society proceedings, send e-mail to cs.books@computer.org or write to Proceedings, IEEE Computer Society, P.O. Box 3014, 10662 Los Vaqueros Circle, Los Alamitos, CA 90720-1314. Telephone +1 714-821-8380. FAX +1 714-761-1784.

Additional information regarding the Computer Society, conferences and proceedings, CD-ROMs, videos, and books can also be accessed from our web site at http://computer.org/cspress

8/24/98